The Girl Who Was No Kin to the Marshalls and Other Stories

by

ANNE HOBSON FREEMAN

With illustrations by
Louise Gilbert Freeman

Dementi Milestone Publishing
Manakin-Sabot, Virginia

The following stories were originally published in:

The Virginia Quarterly Review:

"The Girl Who Was No Kin to the Marshalls;"
"A Question of Timing;"
"At the Museum;"
"Hugh."

Commonwealth:
"Christos Voskrese"

Cosmopolitan:
"About Louise"

McCall's:
"Whatever Happened to Agnes Mason?"

From Mt. San Angela:
"The Fence"

The New Virginia Review:
"The Gift"

Poetry East:
"War Hero"

The following article was originally published in:
Style Weekly: "Willoughby Spit"

ISBN 978-1-7368989-5-6

Editor and Book Designer: Beverly L. Nelson

Dementi Milestone Publishing, Inc., Manakin-Sabot, Virginia 23103
Printed in the United States

For
Elizabeth Seydel Morgan,
my companion in literary escapades
for the past sixty years

CONTENTS

The Girl Who
Was No Kin
to the Marshalls

It began back at her birth, or at least her baptism, when she was named Clare Colston for the mother of her Richmond grandmother. Although this fact endeared her to her relatives in Richmond, it endangered her in Lexington, a dark, alien, and mountainous land ruled by her other grandmother, Margaret Lewis Marshall Marshall. The grandmother for whom Clare's older sister, Maggie, was named.

Every June their parents used to dump the two of them up there while they tootled off for two weeks of vacation

— two bleak weeks for Clare, two blissful weeks for her sister, who could do no wrong in Lexington just as surely as Clare could do no right.

If there was one thing in the world that Grandma Marshall could not abide, it was a child who was timid, a child who hid tear-splotched postcards from her mother underneath her pillow, a child who slunk around the halls, jumping back as if she had just seen a snake when her own grandmother happened to walk past her, and worst of all, perhaps, a child who would come creeping in, in the middle of the night, and tiptoe all the way around the enormous walnut sleigh bed her grandparents slept in to wake up her grandfather, whispering, "Come help me. Please. I can't make the water stop running in the john."

The madder Grandma got, the more timid Clare got. Finally, one Easter night when they were visiting there, as Clare lay in bed she heard her grandmother saying to her mother downstairs:

"Mark my words. You are making a mistake to let that child grow up sensitive and timid. Which is just plain self-centered, if you ask for my opinion. How can you expect her to develop any backbone?"

Clare's mother murmured something.

Then Grandma's voice, strong and clear again: "Of course she can't help the fact she's so much less attractive than her sister. Who has inherited the Marshall coloring..." (That meant dark, curly hair. And fair, rosy skin.)... "while Clare," she was saying, "is like all of the

Colstons" (Clare's father's family)... "Blond and pale and pasty. Every time I look at her I think, 'That child can not be kin to me.'"

At the breakfast table, during those interminable visits in June, Clare would stare into her plate, the Blue Willow pattern, trying to imagine she was halfway round the world from Lexington and Grandma, standing on that tiny bridge with those tiny Chinese people who, she could tell from a certain apologetic hunch in their posture, were every bit as sensitive and timid as the Colstons. She would stare into her plate so that she wouldn't have to look at all the portraits and the photographs of dark-haired, rosy-skinned, flashing blue-eyed Marshalls, lined up on the walls, like an infantry division, backing Grandma up.

Actually, the least ferocious-looking Marshall in the bunch was the old Chief himself, his leathery face webbed with tiny wrinkles. But at least some of them looked like laugh wrinkles. And what she took to be his napkin was tucked into his collar, as if he were expecting to sit down to breakfast, too.

Way down by the sideboard, over Granddaddy's shoulder, there was even more significant visual relief. A steel engraving of Robert E. Lee — full face in his double-buttoned uniform, with soft white hair and beard and eyes that twinkled with a quality she read as sympathy, since he, too, was no kin to the Marshalls.

A slight exaggeration. You would have had to go a long way in Virginia to find a person who was absolutely no kin to the Marshalls. But General Lee was distant kin, at best. As were the poor old Colstons. And heaven knows her grandmother had made it very clear that didn't count.

After they had sat for what seemed several hours at the breakfast table, Grandma would pick up a brass belle (literally, a tiny lady with a clapper under her hoop skirt) and ring for the maid to clear the table.

The maid was a robust, dirty-blonde, pink-kneed girl from Hogback Mountain with a reputation on the campuses of Washington & Lee and V.M.I. that Clare's high-minded grandmother chose simply to ignore.

Her name, it just so happened, was Virginia. And she would bump open the swinging door with one enormous haunch, turn and glare at Grandma with her freckled arms folded on her bosom and say, "What d'ya want?"

"You may clear the table now, Virginia," Grandma would answer with a sigh indicating she would never, ever, quite recover from her dislocation from the better-mannered colored maids of Norfolk and the genteel customs of Tidewater in general where people drove around in "cyars," and cultivated "gyardens" and sometimes even tried to dignify their "gyarbage."

As they pushed their rickety Victorian chairs back from the table, Grandma would train her steel-blue eyes on Clare and say, "It's time for you to walk your grandfather to V.M.I."

Released, at last, Clare would bound out to the sitting room to fetch his leather pouch and pipe, while he'd unhook his khaki officer's cap from the coat rack in the hall, and off the two of them would go. Never once did she question the necessity of walking her grandfather to work. Or ask why her sister was kept at home with Grandma. All she ever wondered, every now and then, was how Grandaddy got to work when she was gone.

By that time he was treasurer of The Virginia Military Institute, a job his friends and cousins got him in the early 1930's when his small bank, the Bank of Tidewater, in Norfolk failed.

As the screen door slammed behind them, she would slip her fingers into her grandfather's rough tobacco-stained hand, and they would cross Washington Street, then step onto the bright white cement walk that ran, like a hem, along the bottom of the lush green lawn of Washington & Lee.

Now Grandaddy was a Marshall, too, of course. He was, in fact, her grandmother's double second cousin. And Clare always assumed, though nobody ever told her, that the main reason Grandma married him was so she wouldn't have to change her maiden name.

But Grandaddy didn't seem like a Marshall. Not Grandma's kind of Marshall anyway, which Clare came to understand later was a relatively rare kind — a City Marshall, fully urbanized, even worse, Tidewaterized. While Grandaddy was a Country Marshall, the more common kind that grew up poor as church mice in Fauquier County right after the Civil War and rode a horse or mule five miles a day to a two-room schoolhouse to acquire a fairly modest education.

Of course she didn't understand these distinctions back in those years when she was eight and nine and ten. All she understood was that if Grandma was a Marshall, then Grandaddy was different, thank the Lord. He seemed to have no standards where people were concerned, liked practically everybody that he ever met. Up to, and including, her.

So she could forget her troubles as she walked along beside him, taking two short steps to every one of his sharp-creased khaki strides, while that huge green hill of Washington & Lee, crowned with white pillared buildings, striped with bright white ribbon walkways, revolved like the canopy of a giant merry-go-round above them.

By the time they had climbed up through the gates of V.M.I. and onto the Parade Ground she would be giddy with relief, saying absolutely anything that came into her head. But then it would be time for Grandaddy to lean down and give her a whiskery, tobacco-smelling kiss and disappear into one of those crenelated, taffy-colored castles. And there he had to stay till one o'clock when she could come to fetch him back for lunch and a game of croquet or maybe Rummy.

In the meantime, there was a whole morning before her. She would turn around then and pick her way back along the edge of the Parade Ground trying not to notice the bruise-purple mountains hovering above her, like the pictures of the Marshalls at the dining room table, trying not to wonder what her sister and her grandmother were planning.

Soon after she had dropped back down the cement walkway into Washington & Lee, she would pass Lee Chapel, just about the time the two ladies who worked there would be propping open its bright, white double doors. The wonderful thing was that she didn't have to pay to get into the Lee Chapel and Museum. All she had to do was say, "Major Marshall's grandchild," words that worked exactly like "Open Sesame." Looking back, she suspected that they must have had a policy of free admission for the families of both college faculties. But back then she was convinced that the miracle was rooted in the awesome power of the Marshall name (a power she could borrow now and then and use on innocent outsiders, who didn't understand the paradoxes of genetics, but a power she could obviously never really own).

Though the lady at the table with the tinted postcards was used to her by now, Clare still felt obliged to mumble "Major Marshall's grandchild," and the lady would then press her lips together, nod, and say, "Make yourself at home."

Which is exactly what she did.

Pushing open the inside door she would step into the cool, clean, absolutely empty chapel, with its bright white walls and curving ceilings, its long white wooden benches lined up in review before the platform where General Lee was sleeping on his marble camp bed with his marble Army boots (square-toed ones she noticed, not round-toed like Grandaddy's) sticking out from underneath his too short marble Army blanket.

She remembered best one drizzly morning, the last week of their visit in 1944. She had a book with her that day, *The Adventures of Tom Sawyer*, so she slipped into a pew and read there till her back began to ache. Then she walked up on the stage, through the archway in the center, and plopped down on the floor beside Lee's statue. The light for reading was wonderful back there, coming as it did through a window on the side and reflecting directly off the marble. And she felt so at ease beside that gentle, sleeping man.

As irony would have it — she had even managed one day to get Grandma to admit it — General Lee was better born than the Marshalls. So much better that he didn't have to worry about who took after who. She had heard one of the ladies explaining to a tourist that Lee liked all his students, no matter who they were or where they came from. And he liked children, too. She took that to mean all of them, even timid ones who weren't but so attractive.

On a warm day she could sit and read beside him for half an hour maybe. (In those days of World War II and gas rationing, it wasn't very often that a tourist would disturb her.) But on this particular day, the hard chill of the marble floor soon worked through her cotton skirt and underpants, so that she had to stand up, and rubbing her behind to restore the circulation, clank on down the iron steps to the museum in the basement

In the hall down there was a photograph of Lee as a civilian in a floppy gray hat, sitting on his horse, Traveller, as relaxed as anybody else would be sitting in an arm-chair. And since Grandma was making Clare take riding lessons every afternoon, she stopped and studied the photograph a while.

"Now that's what I call horsemanship," said the shorter, fatter museum lady, as she passed her standing there.

"What made him so relaxed?" Clare asked.

"Love," the lady said, "Just plain love between a man and animal who'd ridden through so much together. So much dust and rain. And all those muddy, bloody battles. They had learned to communicate like two parts of one body."

Clare couldn't help but notice how loose Lee held his reins. Probably because he didn't even need them. With a slight shift in his weight, or pressure from his leg, he could tell Traveller exactly what he wanted.

After that, Clare wandered down to General Lee's office, which was just as he had left it, the ladies always said, so that visitors could have the feeling that he might be coming back. Maybe that was why Clare could not quite work up the nerve to sit down in his tufted black leather chair and read at his octagon-shaped table.

Instead, she walked on down the hall, took a hard right at the end, and flopped down on her stomach beside the tall glass case that had the skeleton of Traveller inside it. There she set her book down, opened flat, in a rectangle of daylight sifting through a window in the thick white basement wall.

She felt as much at home beside the bones of Traveller as she did upstairs beside the statue of his master. And secretly she longed to break open that case and write her name, Clare Colston, on a chalk white rib, the way so many students had written theirs before her.

It was curious, really, that she felt so much at home there when, at that point in her life, the thing that scared her most, next to Grandma, was horses. Live horses, of course. With long, enormous muscles and sweat-soaked, smelly skin. Horses that could bite your fingers off, if you didn't hold your palm perfectly flat when you offered them a carrot. Horses that could get *mad* and lay their ears back flat and give a mean kick sideways, the way her sister's would, as he cantered past her and poor old Buck.

Buck was what they gave her at the V.M.I. stables, a swaybacked veteran from the cavalry of World War I (when they were in the midst, of course, of World War II). A sweet-natured, gentle thing. Terrified as she was of all horses in general, she could not help acknowledging that fact about old Buck. And things would have been all right if her grandmother had been content to let her walk and trot and, maybe every now and then, canter. But Grandma was a pusher, bound and determined that each child would go home with a skill she had lacked at the time she was committed to her care. And that third summer of lessons, when Grandma noticed Clare had managed, finally, to learn to walk and trot and canter, she insisted it was time for her to JUMP.

Clare was so alarmed when her grandmother announced the plan at breakfast that she actually talked back to her for once: "Oh, why, Grandma? Why? Can't I just pull Buck over to the side and let Maggie and White Lightning take the jumps?"

"Are you afraid to jump?"

"Yes," she said. "I am."

"Then don't you see? That that's the very reason you have to learn to do it."

No, she didn't see. But she was more afraid of Grandma than she was of jumping. And for that reason she began to jump.

One afternoon of that last week in 1944, a day or two after the rainy morning in Lee Chapel, she was trotting Buck up to a three-foot rail that she had taken fairly easily before. But this time, at the last minute, Buck shifted his footing, and Clare bumped out of the saddle as well as both her stirrups, and took the jump straddling his neck.

As Buck came down to the ground and started cantering around the bend, Clare felt herself falling in that awful stretched-out time of a slow-motion movie. First, she tipped over sideways and began slipping down the horse's side (the side facing the ring, thank heavens, not the stucco wall). Then she found herself hanging with one leg hooked over the horse's neck, the other leg swinging free under his stomach. And her head was down there, too, turned and watching, with a curious detachment, as the back hooves did a fancy dance sideways to avoid stepping on her as she fell.

What she felt a second later, sitting in the dust without a scratch or bruise on her, was not fear but gratitude to Buck.

"Are you hurt?" Grandma called from the bench where she was sitting, her black shoes pressed together, her face crumpled into wrinkles as she looked into the sun.

"No," said Clare, standing up and brushing the dust off the jodhpurs, two sizes too big, they had borrowed from the daughter of a Captain Somebody who taught mathematics.

"Then you know what you have to do now. Don't you?"

"Yes," Clare said, "I have to get back up on Buck. And take the jump again."

During all of this, the corporal in charge of the V. M. I, stables, the person who was meant to be giving them their lessons, had not said a word.

Clare walked over to Buck, who was standing waiting for her with his long reins drooping. First, she ran her hand down his sweat-soaked neck, to thank him. Then she gathered up the reins, stuck her toe in the stirrup, and pulled herself up into the saddle.

The wonder of it was that she still wasn't feeling scared. If anything, she felt apologetic. Because she knew if she'd been riding right, with her weight down in her heels, with her thighs and knees and calves clinging to Buck's sides, the way that Lee rode Traveller, she would not have lost her balance in the first place.

After they got home and took their baths, Maggie went

off to the movies with a girl she knew from camp, leaving Clare to spend the rest of the afternoon alone with Grandma.

As they walked downtown to get some meat for dinner, Clare didn't speak to Grandma, because, as usual, she couldn't think of anything to say. But as her grandmother was pushing open the door into the butcher's shop, she said to Clare out of the blue: "I was proud of you today."

It was as if Grandma had given her a diamond, and Clare took that little piece of praise and turned it over in her mind to get every single glint of glory from it. She felt absolutely radiant with glory, as she stood beside the slanted white and glass meat counter, watching the butcher trim the fat from the pork chops, watching Grandma tear a coupon from the perforated sheet in her meat ration book.

But then, two minutes later, she was in trouble again. Her grandmother had just dropped the pork chops into her string shopping bag and was looking down at her: "What would you like to do now?"

"Oh me. I don't know," Clare said, suddenly impaled on this unexpected question. What was she supposed to say? If she said she wanted to do something Grandma didn't want to do. Oh, dear. What would happen then? "I don't know," she said again.

"How can anybody *not know* what they want to do?"

The finely wrinkled skin on Grandma's neck was getting red. Which meant, of course, that she was getting mad at her. So Clare looked down at the floor and began to trace an arc in the sawdust with her sandal, trying to keep back the tears she could feel coming on, tears that would make Grandma FURIOUS at her.

Suddenly she felt her grandmother's fingers lifting up her chin.

"Try to think of me." Grandma's bright blue eyes were boring into hers now, so she couldn't look away. "You're not being fair to me. What I want to do is what you want to do. But there's no way I can do it, if you keep on being shy and hiding what you think from me."

So Clare took a deep breath and blurted out, "Can you take me to the Library to get another book?"

"Of course I can, but I took you there on Tuesday. You checked out *The Adventures of Tom Sawyer*. I thought at the time it was too advanced for you. Is that the problem? It's too long?"

"I've finished it," Clare said.

"Well, good for you," Grandma said. And then, she let go of Clare's chin, but still looked straight into her eyes and added, "I'll say this for the Colstons. I always did hear that they were smart."

A Question of Timing

"How about another drink?" Peter says to the out-of-town lawyer he has brought home unexpectedly for dinner. And he plucks the empty glass out of the man's hand.

"A short one," he explains to me, "while you're putting dinner on the table."

"But dinner's *on* the table. That's what I came to tell you."

"Then take it off," he says and walks over to the bar.

I follow, whispering, since I don't want to make a scene before the tall, skinny stranger from a Wall Street law firm, who is standing by the bookcase, staring like a startled squirrel.

"For God's sake, Peter. It's already ten to seven. They want the speakers on the stage by eight o'clock."

"Relax," he says, tonging ice cubes from the silver ice bucket his groomsmen gave him — good grief, was it just five years ago? "If we eat at seven you'll have ample time to get there."

He says all this out loud, forcing me to make a choice: Nasty scene before his guest? Or complete capitulation. He's got me and he knows it. I cannot bring myself to spill my ugly thoughts before a guest.

So I cork them in my skull and glare at Peter, thinking: damn you and your extra drink. Don't you know that blows it? Blows the fragile schedule I've been building like a cardhouse all day long: Bath at two o'clock while the children are still napping. Park from three to five. Baby down again by six. And dinner on the table by six-fifty at the latest. Now thanks to you, everything will be off balance. Nothing will go right tonight, because I've lost that extra time I need to get my notes arranged before my hands start shaking. To comb my hair if necessary right before I step out on the stage.

Big deal, you would say. A 20-minute talk on Richmond architecture at your old school. Why should you be nervous? A good question, actually. Why am I so jittery? I used to stand up on that stage without a qualm... "Would you like a drink, too?" I hear Peter asking me.

"No!" I say. And then I turn and walk back toward the

kitchen, hammering my heels into the heart-pine floor-boards. One of the main reasons we hocked our souls to buy this hundred-year-old town house. Dirt-smeared, grit-caked, splintery floor boards. One of the main reasons I hate the house now.

As I pass through the tiny dining room, I snatch the casserole from the silver trivet my great-uncle gave us, take four long steps into the narrow pullman kitchen, yank the oven door open, and shove the casserole inside. "I'll be lucky," I am thinking as I slam the oven door and spin the dial to Warm, "damned lucky if I make it to the school by eight o'clock."

"I'm hungry, Mumma," Courtney whines. She is sitting on the kitchen floor playing with the strainer and the soup ladle I gave her earlier to shut her up. Her small back propped against the yellow kitchen wall. Her short, plump legs in their lime green tights jutting out into the space between the wall and the refrigerator door. No shoes on, I notice. Dammit, where'd she leave her shoes?

"Can I have a cookie, Mumma? Can I? Can I have a cookie?" And then she starts to cough. A deep, phlegmy cough. It's getting worse, I think, as I snatch a cookie from the Meissen plate I've brought out for the guest. And that wind in the park didn't do her any good. I hand the cookie down to her. If she's any worse tomorrow, I'll take her to the doctor.

"Move over," I say. "So I can get the butter."

Courtney bites into the cookie and wriggles toward the stove to leave some room for the refrigerator door to open. I grab its metal handle. But the kettle starts to whistle. So I let the handle go and step across the bright green, bump-kneed legs to get back to the stove. "Can't you see you're in the way?" I snap. "Why don't you go into the living room and play?"

"It's cold out there," she says.

She's absolutely right. It is freezing in this house. We keep the thermostat at sixty-two for fear of going bankrupt from the oil bill.

By now the kettle's screaming. Loud. As I would like to scream. So I grab its plastic handle and yank it from the glowing coil.

Right away the screaming stops. And silence. Cool, clean silence washes down the kitchen's narrow, grease-stained, high-gloss yellow walls.

My hands are trembling, I notice, as I start to pour the water into the top half of the old drip coffeepot I bought when I was still in Cambridge, working at the Fogg Museum. It wobbles just a little. I ought to twist it in tighter. But I need two hands to do that. And where can I put the kettle? If I put it on the counter it will burn the Formica. If I put it on the burner, the one free burner, then the scream, that awful scream, will come again. So I do the best I can to twist the top half tight with one hand and continue pouring with the other. When the top is almost full, it tilts, all of a sudden. And spills the boiling water to the floor.

A transparent tongue of water barely misses my skirt and hits the floor, thank the Lord, just this side of Courtney. Then I watch the puddle stretch into a finger pointing straight at Courtney's lime green tights. It would serve Peter right if we killed ourselves out here, I am thinking as I stand there. Frozen. The kettle in my hand. The water finger inching toward the lime green tights.

Suddenly Courtney screams. A scream of pain. Real pain. I drop the kettle on the coil, and it starts screaming, too, as I convert my hands to hooks that scoop the child up at the armpits. And swing her, wet legs flapping, into the dining room where there is a chair that I can sit on while I stand her on my lap and start to pull the steaming green tights off. As I peel the tights down, the skin peels after them, rolling down her chubby legs like a thin pink film of rubber.

And now I'm screaming, too: "Help me! Please. *Somebody*, help me!"

The men come running, then. Their extra drinks still in their hands.

By the time they get to us, Courtney has stopped screaming. She is only sobbing now, her face against my shoulder. I can feel warm tears and mucus soaking through my blouse.

The men's eyes open wide at the sight of the raw red backs of Courtney's legs.

"I spilled the boiling water for the coffee," I begin. "It hit the floor, and got on Courtney's tights ..." And then I stop. Because I realize that words aren't going to help us.

The men are silent, too, as they stand there, helpless sticks against the dining room wall, lamp posts observing the scene of the accident below them while I hold the child against my shoulder and pat her on the back as if she were a baby and she needed burping. All my thoughts and energies are funneled for one moment into this single task.

It is as if the web of words I keep suspended in my skull has been, all of a sudden, swept aside. And I have to act without it. And I feel, to my surprise, more competent without it. Not yanked from thought to thought, but at peace, for once, with everyone around me.

Even with my husband. So far not a word has passed between us. Not a single accusation. Or counter-accusation. Is it possible we realize it doesn't really matter who is finally at fault? All that matters is the child. The life outside our tangled lives that we started once and now have harmed. Oh God, is what I think. Is anybody *sane* enough to be a decent parent?

Then I notice Peter's arms. Stretched out to take Courtney. "Can I hold her for you? While you call the doctor?"

He's afraid to call himself. I feel, unexpectedly, a rush of sympathy for him. "Yes," I say, and hand him up his raw-legged, sobbing daughter and walk out to the hall and dial Dr. Henderson who is, thank the Lord, at home.

"How extensive are the burns?" he asks.

"All over her legs."

"Be *specific!*" he shouts back.

"Down the backs of both her legs," I try to keep my voice level, "from her buttocks to her ankles," and feel suddenly pleased, what a strange time to be pleased, with myself for thinking up a word as anatomical and accurate as "buttocks."

There is silence for a second. Then the doctor's husky voice. Calm now and not angry. Steady as a hand holding up my elbow. "Cover up the legs with towels," he says. "Clean turkish towels, to cut down on exposure to infection. That's the danger of a burn. Once a large part of the body has been stripped of its protective armor, infection is liable to take over. So keep her legs covered with the towels. And put an ice pack on them, if she'll tolerate the ice. And get her to the Medical College right away."

In the meantime he will call ahead and get the burn specialist, Dr. Yates, to meet us in the Burn Ward.

The guest agrees to look after the baby if he wakes. So we leave him there, poor man. We hardly even know him. Leave him sitting on the sofa, sipping on his second drink.

Peter drives while I sit in the back with Courtney, who is lying on her stomach with her legs across my lap. Every time I try to press the ice pack to the burns, she cries, "Don't. Don't! It *hurts*!"

Finally, I give up and simply drape the towels across her legs. We drive on, then, in silence. And my mind begins projecting, in the darkness of the car, a Kodachrome slide show — beach shots of Courtney as a teenager with sausage-withered legs sticking out of her bikini. ...

So I force myself to look out of the windshield. And see that we are now downtown. Turning right on Broad Street where the ruby red taillights of the cars in front of us are spilling like a necklace into Shockhoe Valley, where the town of Richmond started, and up the distant hill to St. John's Church. On the other side of Broad I see a chain of white lights moving toward us. Down the slope of Church Hill. And up the slope of this hill, which is Court Hill, where George Wythe lived and died (poisoned by his nephew). And John Marshall built his house. And now the Medical College has put up skyscrapers, jagged teeth planted in the hillside.

I can see the Main building ahead of us now, with a searchlight on its tower that goes up and out, revolving. A flat finger of light accusing something way up in the sky.

In the Admissions Office the aluminum ball on the electric typewriter types out line after line of names, addresses, numbers, while I shift Courtney's weight from one hip to the other and readjust the towels to cover her legs completely, to keep out all the germs that must be floating in this office.

Peter searches through his wallet for the Blue Cross card. Finds it. Hands it to the woman. And the metal ball types that number, too. Then pecks a little sentence of its own:

"Mother alleges child was accidentally burned by boiling water."

Rrrip. The woman yanks the form out of the typewriter. Tears a sheet from it. Hands it up to Peter. "Take this to the Burn Ward. Elevator on your right to the third floor."

As soon as we step out into the Burn Ward, a typist traps Peter. And a nurse beckons to me — I am still carrying Courtney, still struggling to keep the skirt of towels on her legs — and leads us down a hall to a clean white cubicle where a sterile sheet has been spread on an examining table. Apparently she wants me to set Courtney down on it. So I tip her body forward, slide one hand beneath her knees so that her legs won't have to bend. What hurts her most of all is when her legs are forced to bend. Then I lower her gently to the table on her stomach.

The nurse draws back the towels and studies Courtney's legs. The skin is pink now, in most places, with periodic puddles of dark red.

"Not as bad as I expected," says the nurse. "Mostly first degree. Some second. Few, if any, third."

She bends down to speak to Courtney, who is lying with her face flattened sideways on the table. Eyes wide open. Staring straight ahead. "I wouldn't be surprised if Dr. Yates lets you go home tonight, young lady."

The nurse's rubber soles pivot then, and squeak out of the room. I follow her into the hall. "Will the burns leave scars?"

"I don't know," says the nurse. "Dr. Yates can tell you that."

So I step back into the cubicle and wait.

Peter sticks his head in. "How ya doin', Pooh?"

"Fine," Courtney says. But only her lips move.

Since the room's too small for all of us, Peter says he'll wait, lamp post witness once again, out in the hall.

A medical student ambles in with a syringe tucked under the fingers of the hand that he keeps casually by his side. With his free hand he pulls back Courtney's jumper and exposes her bare bottom. Swabs it with a dot of cotton. Then, Zip. The needle's Up. And In. And Out. Before she has a chance to cry.

"Tetanus," he explains as he wipes the needle clean.

I now hear plastic casters rolling on the tile floor of the hall and I turn and see a stretcher sliding past the doorway. First a tight white sheet, wound around a body. Finally a face. The brown, hooked, flint-nosed profile of a woman. An Indian woman. With her eyes shut tight. Is she dead? I wonder. No — I can see a slight rising and falling in the sheet across her chest.

Behind the stretcher comes an old man. Black. Rocking on his rundown heels. His white hair pressed in tiny coils against his head. His overcoat hanging limply from his bony shoulders. He is carrying a child, a little black girl about a year younger than Courtney.

"His granddaughter," the medical student whispers to me. "The other is his wife." He nods toward the stretcher. "Burned when their oil stove exploded."

The orderlies park the stretcher on the far side of the hall and leave it. Leave the woman sleeping. And gesture to the old man to go into the cubicle opposite Courtney's. I watch him stand the child up on the sterile-sheeted table. Her fat brown baby legs are pumping with impatience. But so far she has not made a single sound.

The entire scene, in fact, is played out in silence as I try not to stare at the peeling pink patches on the child's brown legs and arms, and the red patch on her stomach that is partially covered by a pair of dingy gray training pants.

Oh my God, take them off! I think.

As if he reads my mind, the medical student steps across the hall and reaches for the training pants. But the old man blocks him with his arm. No words pass between them. The student shrugs his shoulders and steps back from the room. Then he walks on down the hall.

Infection! I am screaming somewhere way behind the silence. You should let him take those pants off! Don't you understand about the danger of infection?

But I do not say a word out loud. No one dares to break the silence as we wait there. Together. Propped against the terrifying silence.

Then I hear rubber soles squeaking in the hall. He is coming. Dr. Yates. Like the king in an Elizabethan drama. Hirelings, nurses, interns, rushing down the hall before him. A flurry of activity. And then, the Man, Himself. Bowing into first one tiny room, and then another. Examining the burns. Then muttering instructions which are instantly recorded onto stainless steel clipboards. The woman on the stretcher and the black child, they must stay, he says. And this child. (He is looking now at Courtney's legs.) This child can go home, as soon as she is bandaged.

He turns his face toward me. The kindest, most forgiving face I've ever seen. "Your child will be all right," he says. "There won't be any scars. Except perhaps a small one on her thigh. We'll bandage up her legs now. And give her penicillin. Can you bring her back to see me Tuesday morning at eleven?"

"Yes," I say. "Yes." And then I add, to my surprise — ordinarily I'd realize it really isn't any of my business —

"What about the others?" I nod toward the stretcher.

Dr. Yates presses his lips into a line as thin as string. "We will see," he says. And, oh my God, I know exactly what he means.

Then, before I can say thank you, he is gone.

A nurse and an intern bandage Courtney's legs from her thighs to her ankles, leaving only her feet free. The student with the syringe ambles in again and gives her a shot of penicillin.

"Now she can go home," he says.

"Thank you," I say. "Thank you," while Peter steps into the room and picks up Courtney and holds her by the waist so that I can put her coat on, her green plaid Sunday coat, which now has clean white leggings that stick out straight into the air, as Peter makes a chair out of his arms.

That's how he takes her down the hall, while I follow, tossing words of gratitude like daisies at whatever nurses, orderlies, or interns happen to walk past me in the hall. I feel compelled to give back something for this unexpected gift, this gratuitous release from the punishment I know that I deserve. Scars on Courtney's legs. Lifelong reminders of my failure as a mother.

Oh God, please, I am thinking as we stand and wait for the elevator to come down from the 10th floor. Please help me be a better mother. Yet even as I think this, I know that I won't be. Very possibly I can't be.

When the elevator doors slide open, I let Peter go in first, preceded by Courtney's bright white fork-lift legs.

Then I step inside, myself, and press the lobby button.

As the metal doors slide shut, I glance down at my watch. And see, to my surprise, that it is still only eight twenty-five.

Only eight twenty-five? I can feel my spider mind throwing out a guy line. Probably the first speech isn't even over yet... And I am scheduled fourth ... If I could just persuade Peter to put Courtney to bed, and feed his guest the dinner, I could be out at the school by nine o'clock ...

A reasonable plan. And so I say to Peter, as I begin to feel the elevator moving down, "I think I still have time to give my talk. If you would just put ..."

"No," he says. Calmly, but firmly. "Don't you understand? You can't leave her tonight."

"But they'll never ask me back if I let them down tonight..." I hear my own voice pleading like an engine disengaged from the rest of my mind, which has already decided that I won't leave her tonight. That for once Peter is right. And yet that other part of me keeps on talking: "I've heard they're looking for a teacher. A part-time teacher in the history of art. If I could go there for an hour. Just to give my talk, which is a damn good talk ..."

Then I look across at Courtney, who is staring at me blankly, her thin wrists locked around her father's neck, offering her eyes like plates, Wedgwood blue plates, onto which I can deposit anything I please.

As soon as we get home I phone the school and try to explain to them why I cannot come. Then, while Peter and the lawyer finish up the wine and casserole, I carry

Courtney up the steps — 19 heart-pine steps —into the back bedroom where I stand her on her bed and take her jumper off.

"I have to wee-wee," she says.

A wave of panic washes over me. How can she do that? Without ruining the bandages? Without spraying them with urine which will soak into the burns?

Oh my God, is what I think. Why did I forget to ask the doctor how to do this?

But, "OK" is what I say. Trying to sound confident. As if this were a perfectly acceptable request. "But you've got to wait. Do you hear? Till I get you fixed in just the right position. So you won't wet your bandages. OK?"

"OK," she says.

I can feel the muscles in my forearms straining as I swing Courtney down over the toilet seat, bending my legs slowly, so slowly in fact that I feel one stocking break into a run. I tip her body back against my right arm so the bandaged legs go up and form a V. Then I slide my left hand down her legs to shield the spot way up on her thigh where the bandages stop. Now if any urine splashes there, it splashes on my hand.

I can feel Courtney's wrist bone pressing on my neck-bone. Her warm, sweet breath blowing on my cheek.

"OK You can go," I say.

And then we wait there, locked together. Me kneeling. She hanging. Both absolutely still. And barely breathing. As we used to wait a year ago when she was being trained.

Can she manage it? I wonder. In this strange position?

If I just had one hand free, I could reach around and turn the spigot on. It always used to help her when I turned the spigot on.

Then I hear the sound. The reassuring sound of water pouring into water.

I wait until it stops. Slide my arm across her back to reach the toilet paper. Tear a few sheets off. And blot up any drops of urine there might be between her legs.

"Good girl!" I say. "You didn't get a drop on either bandage."

Instantly I feel Courtney's spine relax against my arm. Her wrist bones tighten at my neck.

"You're my best friend," she says.

And for a while I cannot speak.

As I kneel there, locked in the hug of my warm, defenseless daughter, I can feel the strength draining from my leg muscles. And I wonder for a second where I'm going to find the spurt of energy I'll need to lift the weight of both our bodies up, onto my feet.

Christos Voskrese

Angela Lybrook, former typist at the Museum of Fine
Arts, is waiting on the hillside by the open grave, pulling
the lapels of her new red coat, with its soft black velvet
collar, tighter to her neck to keep out the cold November
wind. She begins to stomp her shoes against the frozen
ground because her toes are getting numb.

Finally, she sees the hearse winding up the hill toward
them, a noiseless needle working through the bare tree
trunks, pulling a thread of cars behind it. When it reaches
the gravesite, it stops. Two stone-faced attendants swing
back the double doors and the casket erupts into the gray
morning, spilling the brilliant colors of the Ukrainian Na-
tional Flag.

How inappropriate for Mr. Lubansky, she thought. He
always worked so hard to disappear into his surround-
ings. She can see him now, standing at the entrance to

the Egyptian Gallery, as immobile as the statues that he guarded, his immense chest swelled under the silver buttons of his dark blue uniform, all light quenched behind his steel-rimmed spectacles so that nobody would notice that he was, in fact, alive.

Wouldn't such a man have preferred a plain gray coffin, inconspicuous against the dull gray sky?

But his stubborn, swollen-legged wife had insisted on the flag: "Because he was, how do you say it? A *politische* man. My son, I thank the Lord, is no such man. He will be a good provider. But my husband. Aagh. Cursed he was from the beginning with his love for the Ukraine. And it brought him, I can tell you, nothing but trouble. Trouble with the Bolsheviki. Trouble with the Nazis. Trouble with the Immigration people in New York. How much does a man have to pay to his country? Is it enough, his profession? And his health? And his daughter? It is enough, I say. Mr. Lubansky paid enough. He shall have, please, the flag over his casket."

Angela does not like this woman. Yesterday, when she stopped by to leave her card at the Lubanskys' apartment, out of duty only, the woman insisted that she come inside and sit with her; drew her into that dark and dusty web of relics, paralyzing her with continuous complaints in broken English, even shouting as she left: "You did not know this man. You hear? You knew his ghost!"

Angela watches Mrs. Lubansky now as she swings her heavy legs out of the rented limousine, plants her black oxfords on the ground and rises unsteadily, leaning on the arm of her son who is doing well, she said, making good money in the ball bearing business in New Jersey.

Seeing that the old woman is ready, the undertaker nods, and the pallbearers, most of them guards from the Museum, begin to lug their heavy burden toward the raw cut in the hillside. Mrs. Lubansky stomps heavily behind them, her thick features twisted, not with grief, but with anger. Stubborn, unremitting anger.

As they lower the casket onto the steel brace across the open grave, Angela remembers the first week she came to the Museum, taking the job as typist in School Services although it paid ten dollars a week less than another job she had been offered. "It's worth the sacrifice," her mother said, "because you'll meet nice girls at the Museum. The kind of girls you would have met if you had gone to college."

What Angela could not bring herself to tell her mother was that those "nice girls" didn't waste their time on typists. Three times during her first week there, she set her tray down on the table next to theirs in the staff cafeteria. But they would not break the rhythm of their constant conversation. Yet they would weep, Angela actually saw one of them weep, over photographs of Florence in the flood.

Finally one morning, out of a compulsion to make contact with someone in that vast, indifferent building, Angela gulped down her shyness and spoke to a guard, an immense bespectacled old man who was stationed by the time clock. Somebody had told her he was Russian. And so that morning she said, cheerfully, as if she always spoke to strangers, "Good morning" in Russian: *"Dobry dien."*

Instantly the opaque spectacles flickered with interest. *"Vi govorite po-russki?"*

"No. Not really. But I took Beginning Russian in high school."

"Da. Is good," he said, slipping back behind the curtain of his shyness, and bowing as he did so *"Dobry dien."*

After that Angela and Mr. Lubansky exchanged a greeting every morning, usually in Russian. Now and then he would teach her a phrase, or correct her pronunciation. And that was all there was to it. Until Christmas. Actually a few weeks before Christmas. One night after dinner, Angela's mother handed her a box of Christmas cards. "Why don't you send some of these to those nice girls you work with?"

Expensive cards, Angela noticed with annoyance. Seventy-five cent cards. She decided it was time she made her mother face the fact that there are two kinds of girls who work at the Museum: college graduates who breeze in for short jobs between their trips to Europe and work for the fun of it and lunch with the director; and other girls, like Angela, who work for the money, typing and filing away weeks, then months, then whole years of their lives in fluorescent-lit, cinderblock cells, deprived even of windows from which they might at least have watched the changing seasons.

But when Angela turned to speak to her mother, she caught sight of the hand holding out the box of cards to her. The skin across the thumb was splotched with liver spots. And along the palm, there was a ridge of mustard-colored calluses, from shoveling snow off the front steps, or carrying trays up to what used to be the guest room where Angela's father lay half-paralyzed from a stroke.

And what she found herself saying was: "All right, Mother. I'll send some Christmas cards."

From a mimeographed list of the Museum Staff, Angela began to address Christmas cards to Jane and Clare who did School Tours and occasionally asked her to type up schedules for them. And one to Sarah in Accessions. And, of course, a card to Mrs. Jorgensen, her boss. All four of them, she noticed, had the same stylish zip code. Then her eyes slipped down the page and caught on the name of Mr. Lubansky. She felt a twinge of affection for Mr. Lubansky; he had a semi-slummy zip code, just like hers.

Why not send a Christmas card to him, too? It might mean something to him.

Two days later as Angela punched in at the time-clock, Mr. Lubansky thanked her with moist eyes and profuse and fluent Russian which, unfortunately, Angela could not follow. Then, three months later, in the mail, an Easter card arrived with a greeting printed in Russian and the simple signature, "L. J. Lubansky."

When Angela pulled the card out of the envelope, three pressed flowers fell into her hand.

The Museum was closed on Easter Monday. But on Tuesday Angela thanked Mr. Lubansky. He bowed a deep, formal bow and explained that for the next forty days he would greet her with *"Christos voskrese"* which meant "Christ is risen," and she must reply with *"Voistynu voskrese* (He risen indeed)."

When the forty days were up, they went back to *"dobry dien"* again and gradually spring passed into summer and summer into winter with Angela typing through the days and watching TV through the nights until occasionally, in moments of depression, she began to think the "dings" of the margin bell and the "bongs" of the station breaks were tolling the passing of her life.

It wasn't that she didn't like being a typist. She actually enjoyed it. Some days she could work herself into a trance where the words slipped through her fingertips without a single interruption from her brain.

December came around again. And there she was at her second Staff Christmas Party, smiling mechanically, in every direction, while her hands burned large and awkward at her side. How soon could she leave, she wondered, without seeming to be rude? Then she saw Mr. Lubansky standing straight and stiff against the cinderblock wall, his blue eyes glazed with fright behind the steel-rimmed spectacles. And she forgot her own discomfort and walked across the room to speak to him.

All he gave her in return was a small, abrupt nod of recognition. When she did not go away, he began to shift his weight from foot to foot. Finally, he shouted down to the gray head of the woman at his side: "My friend, Miss Lybrook!"

"Mrs. Lubansky," he explained to Angela. And once

again he was silent, though he smiled a slim smile to convey his sorrow that in the present circumstances, he knew she would excuse him, this was absolutely all that he could manage.

A few seconds later the smile had vanished and Mr. Lubansky was standing as stiff as she had found him, so Angela turned to his wife and tried to start a conversation. As it happened, she had just been reading the letters of Stalin's daughter in one of her mother's magazines, and so she shouted to the Russian woman, above the roar of conversation:

"Have you read Svetlana's letters? The letters of Stalin's daughter?"

"Svetlana?" the woman shouted back at her. "Vat do I think of this Svetlana? I despise this woman. Why should she get so much money? She's a D.P. just like me. A million dollars, my son tells me, Svetlana Stalin gets for one small book. My husband writes three books. You come to my apartment. I will show you. Big thick books. He writes in Russian. Aagh, this Svetlana. Why should she get so many dollars for one small book?"

What a woman Angela thought. No wonder poor Mr. Lubansky sought refuge in the Museum's tomb-like silence broken only by the squeaking of his shoes and the tapping of his heels on the marble floor.

Early in the New Year Mr. Lubansky was shifted from his old place by the time-clock to the Galleries upstairs and after that, Angela hardly ever saw him. She did not like to go up into the Galleries. She felt uncomfortable around all of those paintings by men whose names she did not know how to pronounce

Gradually the days at the Museum merged into weeks and the weeks into months till it was time for spring again. Angela noticed it one day in March as she was walking back from lunch. The silhouette of an oak tree leapt into her field of vision, its thick trunk spreading up into a tangled ball of twigs that looked exactly like a lung turned upside down. As Angela moved closer to the tree, she could see that the twigs were swollen tight with sap. The air was different, too. Warmer, heavier and sweeter. She took a swallow of it and felt that there was going to be a change.

When she got back to her desk there was a note for her to go to Mrs. Jorgensen's office. Right away.

"Angela," said Mrs. Jorgensen in a flat Midwestern voice that allowed no contradiction, "I want you to take the Easter Tour for the rest of the week. Starting tomorrow morning. In the Fabergé collection."

"Why *me?*" Angela asked. "I don't know a thing about the Fabergé collection."

"But at least you know your way through the Museum. I'm sorry, Angela, but there's no one else to do it. As you know, Clare is in France. And Jane called in today to say she has the flu. It isn't difficult," she added, her taut face relaxing slightly. "And Mr. Lubansky says that you can do it."

"Mr. Lubansky?"

"I spoke to him this morning, hoping he would give in

just this once and do a tour for me. You know he used to be a professor back in the Ukraine. And an art collector, too. But he had some awful shock, during World War II, and refuses to have contact with the public. He turned me down today, as he has always done, but then he suggested that I might get you to do it."

"He doesn't understand," Angela protested. "He doesn't realize I haven't been to college."

"Why don't you go upstairs and talk to him?" Mrs. Jorgensen said, as she began to shift the papers on her desk. "He told me that you and he were friends."

Mr. Lubansky worked with Angela for almost two hours in the Fabergé collection. First, he identified the faces of the Czar's family, lean, aristocratic faces smiling from bejeweled frames that were delicately filigreed in gold and silver. Then he gave her the names of the semi-precious stones from which Fabergé's craftsmen had carved the tiny rabbits and the miniature flowers and the elaborate Easter eggs which the Czar presented every year to his wife and to his mother.

"Olga and Anastasia. Lapis lazuli and alabaster..." The exotic syllables seemed to slip from Angela's memory as fast as Mr. Lubansky pronounced them. A wave of panic splashed over her. How could she talk about these things tomorrow if she couldn't remember any of their names?

"It's no use!" she wailed. "How can I give a tour when I don't know a thing about Russian history? Or Fabergé? Or art?"

Mr. Lubansky tucked his chin into the folds of his neck

and stared at Angela over the rims of his round steel spectacles. His eyes — unmasked at last — were cool blue flames.

"Can you read, Miss Lybrook?" he said levelly.

"Of course I can read."

"Then tell me, please, why you cannot learn what is in books?"

"It's not that easy," Angela snapped back. "It isn't all written down in books. And even if it was, a person would need training to be able to find it." Angela was angry now. Only one time in her life had anybody else suggested she was lazy. The guidance counselor in high school. But everybody knew he was a fool.

Are you saying that I'm lazy? If you want to know the truth, I think you're the one who's lazy. You've already got all that knowledge in your head and you refuse to take the tour."

"Please," he said. "Will you speak more slowly?"

So she slowed down then and spat the words out, one by one. "Why don't *you* give the tour: You know it all already. Why should I have to do it, if you won't?"

"Wait," he said. "Let me see if I understand the thing that you are saying. An old man cannot do it. And this is the reason that a young girl should not try?"

Angela did not answer him. She left him. Stomped out of the Gallery, down the red-carpeted staircase and back into her cinderblock office. But later, on her way out of the building that evening, she checked out several books on Peter Carl Fabergé.

By the time she finished her first tour the next morning, Angela's anger had subsided. After all, she had survived it. For thirty minutes straight she had managed to keep talking, and though her voice was hoarse, her hopes were high as climbed the red-carpeted staircase back up to the Galleries to hear what Mr. Lubansky thought of her performance.

"I am your friend, no? And from a friend comes the truth. You had too many facts today. It is good you have been reading. But tomorrow, please think about the children. Do not smother their first wonder with your facts. Give them, please, a little time to look and see and touch. And after that, I promise, they will ask you for your facts."

The next day Angela did her best to follow his advice. But with twenty children running from display case to display case, jabbing fingers, pressing noses on immaculate glass cases, she found it hard to suppress the impulse to control them. Wasn't it against the rules to let them touch the glass? ("And who is to know?" said Mr. Lubansky. "They leave marks on the glass? I have a handkerchief. I wipe them off.")

After she had seen the children safely to the school bus, Angela came back upstairs and found Mr. Lubansky leaning over a display case, rubbing off the smudges with his large white handkerchief. As he straightened up to speak to her, she noticed he was wheezing. And his face was unusually red.

"Are you all right?" she asked.

"Da. It's just old age," he said. "Today was better, no?

Today I think the children will remember."

"Maybe so," said Angela.

"Tomorrow," he said, "when the children ask about the eggs, tell them of the Russian Easter. How we use the eggs and gifts to celebrate the Resurrection, and the coming of spring. First, I think you must explain to them the Russian winter. How everything is frozen there. And afternoons are dark as night and heavy on the soul. They must know about our winter, eh? To understand the ecstasy at Easter."

So the next day Angela tried to explain about the Russian Easter, glancing now and then at Mr. Lubansky who, as usual, offered her absolutely no support in public. He simply stood there, frozen in the doorway, all light quenched behind his steel-rimmed spectacles. At one point Angela was tempted to blurt out to the children: "Ask that guard over there. He's Russian. He can tell you all about it." But in the end, she resisted the betrayal. And when the tour was over, she filed the children past him, silently. Only one of them, she noticed even glanced up at his face.

Two weeks later Mrs. Jorgensen stopped at Angela's desk. "Take a look at this," she said handing her a sheet of paper with the letterhead: Crestwood School. An art teacher had written that last week's tour of the Fabergé collection was one of the best she could remember. She wanted to request the same guide, Angela Lybrook, when she brought her seventh grade next Tuesday.

"See. You're not so bad," Mrs. Jorgensen said as she

took the letter back. "Did you know Clare's getting married?"

"No," said Angela. Nobody had told her.

"And it may be several months before I can replace her. So I want you to learn the Egyptian Tour, too. Jane, I think, can handle all the others." Then Mrs. Jorgensen put one hand on her hip, cocked her head and stared at Angela. "You know, there's no reason why you shouldn't go after that job. You could sign up for some courses at the Evening College, and work toward a degree in History of Art. I might even get the Museum to pay tuition for you."

Even now six months later, Angela is wondering how it all started. At what precise point in time did the change begin? The day she swallowed her shyness and spoke to Mr. Lubansky? Or the day he made her angry? Anger is at least a sign of life.

Even the anger of Mrs. Lubansky.

As her mind drifts back into the present, Angela finds that she is staring at Mrs. Lubansky, who is now holding the flag, a folded triangle of color, against her broad, black bosom, scowling at the priest as he sprinkles words over the casket, leaning still on the arm of her dough-faced son.

"He did not understand his son," she said yesterday at the apartment. But how he loved his daughter! Poetry they read together while we shivered in Vienna and waited for our visas. Pushkin. While my son and I, we went into the streets and found the sticks that kept us warm. Aagh.

What good is poetry, I ask you, when the stove is dying? It did not help her, I can tell you, when her cough became pneumonia. She died there in Vienna. Mr. Lubansky told you? She died there in that D.P. camp," she said, "on a stinking bed of straw."

"Is that your daughter?" Angela asked, nodding at a photograph ornately framed in silver — the long, patrician profile of a girl who was almost beautiful. "Such a pretty girl. Is that your daughter?"

"Nyet," the woman said "Dat was myself."

The priest is holding up his hand now for the final words of benediction: "Unto God's gracious mercy and protection we commit you..." and as he speaks, a few leaves float down on the casket, scrape across it, noisily, then somersault into the open pit below.

The priest closes his prayer book. And Angela feels cheated, realizing that they will not see the burial completed, but must leave the coffin there on that efficient and indifferent steel contraption.

Tightening the belt on her bright red coat, she turns away and joins the crowd of mourners as they disperse in silence, walking back to their parked cars, kicking the dried leaves across the frozen ground.

About Louise

Liza's Catholic. So she went into a black box and told her priest about Louise. And that was that for Liza. And he promised he wouldn't tell on her. But I'm Episcopalian, and Lord knows I'd rather die than tell my preacher. I don't know how I'd tell it anyway. Louise was so queer nobody could explain her. I wish I could have heard Liza tell it.

Louise was from New York, I think. Nobody ever said, but she talked like she came from New York. Her grandmother lives in a big brick house on the corner of our block. Her grandfather's dead. Liza and I watched them carry him out on a stretcher, his toes and his nose sticking up through the sheet like little mountains, and the ambulance lights blinking, and Liza's maid, Kate, waving from the porch for us to come away from there.

A few days after that, some strangers drove up in black cars. Louise was in one of those cars, though I didn't see her get out. I was too busy playing jacks with Liza on the sidewalk. The first thing I know, there is Louise, standing right beside us, still and quiet as a bird. Staring down at us with her great big purple eyes.

She had a chopped-off haircut and shiny black bangs. And she wore high socks. Long white socks. I knew right away she was peculiar.

When she saw me looking up at her, she smiled a little

bit and said "Hello?" in this put-on northern voice. I guess I said, "Hi" back. I don't know for certain. I was still so shocked at her appearance.

"Come along, Louise," said a gorgeous blonde lady in a dark blue dress. And that turned out to be Louise's mother. I watched Louise slide her pale white hand into her mother's, a lovely sunburnt hand with painted pink fingernails and heavy gold rings on it. And they began to climb the steep stone steps up to the big house while a chauffeur brought suitcases in behind them.

The next morning somebody called our mothers up and asked if we would please come up to the big house and play with Louise. I didn't like the idea much. But I was glad to get a chance to look inside that house. Liza and I had never had a satisfactory look inside it. In the front they kept the blinds shut most of the time, and in the back there was a big fat maid who would chase us out of the yard, if we had climbed over the wall to get a tennis ball or something.

Anyway, we had to put on dresses. Nobody in our neighborhood wears dresses in the summer. But we had to put them on when we went to see Louise.

My mother rang the doorbell, and Louise's nurse came to the door. A white nurse, if you please, in a white uniform and even white shoes and stockings. The first one we had ever seen outside of a hospital. Right away Liza said she wanted to go home. But Mother made us go inside. She said it would be rude to back out on Louise and that we only had to stay for half an hour. And she let me wear her watch so I could tell when time was up and we could go.

Louise's mother wasn't there. Only the white nurse who said she was going to take us to the sitting room where Louise was waiting for us. "But be gentle with Louise," she said. "She hasn't played with many children."

"How old is Louise?" I asked.

"Eleven," said the nurse.

I looked sideways at Liza. I was eight and a half. And Liza was nine. It seemed to me that nurse was asking the wrong people to be gentle.

Anyway, she led us through the cool, dark hall and then pushed back the sliding doors into the sitting room. It was a great big beautiful room with fancy gold mirrors that began with little marble benches and shot up to the ceiling. And bow-legged tables. And pale blue silk on the chair seats and the sofas. It was old-fashioned all right. But not falling-down old-fashioned like my grandmother's house. I had to strain to see it all because the room was pretty dark. As usual, they had the front blinds shut.

Louise was sitting in the middle of a flimsy little sofa, over by the fireplace.

"Hello, my friends," she said in this gushy northern voice, patting the silk cushion with her pale white hand. "Come here and sit beside me."

It was weird all right. Liza says she knew it when she saw that nurse. I didn't really catch on till I heard Louise talking in that put-on voice of hers. But we made the best of it. And a funny thing happened while we sitting there, crammed down on the flimsy love seat on each side of Louise. Liza asked if she could please have a look at the little gold heart that was hanging on a chain around Louise's neck.

"Do you like it, Eliza?" Louise fiddled with the catch till she undid it. "Then you may have it." She hooked the chain around Liza's neck, a chain that looked like gold, solid gold to me.

"I'll trade you for it," Liza said as she tucked her chin in tight to get a good look at that locket. "I've got some new steel jacks. And a bank that works like a cash register."

"No, no," said Louise in this sad, sad voice. "I want to give it to you. Please, Eliza. Let me give it to you."

"Take it," I said. I had been planning for some time to work up a trade on that cash register, myself.

Louise swung around to me then. "Poor, poor Clare. Did you think I had forgotten you? You're my dear friend, too. Would you like to have a ring?" And with that she pulls off this thin gold ring with a purple birthstone in it, and began to push it on my finger. She had to push it hard because my knuckle's pretty big and has a callus on the side from scraping on the sidewalk, playing jacks. But Louise managed it, at last.

"Thanks, Louise," I said. Then I couldn't help asking, "Do you always give away your stuff to your friends?"

My doctor doesn't let me play with friends at home," she said, "Only Susan and Sally." Then she giggled. "But I can't give them presents."

"Why not?" I asked.

"Because. They're my *imaginary* friends."

See what I mean about Louise?

I asked her if these friends of hers were invisible. And she said no, not exactly. She could see them in her mind. Susie had blonde hair like Eliza's. Sally had brown hair like mine, only curly. She could see them very well when she wanted to see them. But, of course, nobody else could see them.

"Of course," we said. And then we dropped the subject.

We still had fifteen minutes left, so Liza and I made up a game around the box of candy that was sitting on the marble mantelpiece. Louise had given each of us one piece already. But we had to make up the game to get the rest of it.

First, we grabbed our stomachs and rolled off the sofa groaning. Right away Louise fell down on the rug beside us with her white hands on her face, her purple eyes wide open. "Oh, my friends!" she cried. "What has happened to my friends?"

"Only one thing will save us," I said, pointing to the mantlepiece. "A magic pill of candy."

"Quick!" Liza said, "A caramel candy."

Louise understood. She jumped up to her feet and grabbed the box of candy. Then she knelt down beside it on the oriental rug, stroking our foreheads, and periodically popping candy in our mouths.

After five or six caramels, I looked at my watch and saw our time was up and we could go.

When we got back to Liza's house, her mother made us turn right around and take the ring and necklace back. I had suspected all along that that would happen. Louise's nurse came to the door. And she wasn't mad at all. She said she knew Louise had given us those things and weren't we nice to bring them back. And then I watched her drop them, first the locket, then the ring, into the pocket of her nurse's uniform.

A few days after that, Louise came to play with us at Liza's house. The nurse told Liza's mother we were such good playmates she was glad to let her come and play with us.

We decided we'd dress up, since Louise was so good at make believe. Liza, as the Devil, in a red satin cape she wears in her school orchestra recitals, and me, as the Good Fairy, in my sister's powder-blue junior bridesmaid's dress.

I was hiding in the kitchen, with my costume on already, while Liza went and met Louise in her regular clothes and brought her around to the back yard.

First, I heard her offering Louise a drink of papaya juice, this real expensive stuff that comes from Mexico, I think, which Liza's father uses in his drinks. It was meant to be the Evil Potion which would start the whole game going. But wouldn't you know? Louise wouldn't take it.

"No, thank you," she said. "Nana doesn't let me have sweet drinks between my meals."

"You ought to take one sip at least," Liza said. "Or I'll think you're being *rude*."

So Louise said all right, she would take one little sip. And as soon as Liza saw her swallow she said, "OK, that's enough. Now you wait right here and keep your eyes closed, do you hear? While I go into the garage just for a minute."

It was almost time for my appearance now, so I tiptoed up to the screen door where I could see Louise standing by the back porch steps, her eyes shut tight. She was overdressed, as usual, in patent leather shoes, high white socks and a pale purple dress with a big wide fluffy bow. And I noticed that she didn't have on jewelry today.

The more I looked at Louise, the more I thought that she was pretty. If you could forget the stupid haircut and the long, white stocks. She had honest-to-goodness coal-black hair, so clean that it shined, and this thin white skin that you could see the pale blue veins through. I felt kind of sorry for her, standing there beside the steps with her eyes shut tight, expecting something nice.

In fact, I might have stopped the game then, if it hadn't been too late. The garage door was opening. And there was Liza sneaking out of it as the Devil in that bright red satin cape and a black cardboard mustache from a Crackerjack box. She was carrying a wire leaf rake she had found in the garage. One of those long, leaf rakes with shaky, skinny fingers.

Liza slinked up behind her, stuck her rake pole in the ground and called.

"Loueez!"

"Who are you?" cried Louise as she jumped around to face her.

"I'm the Devil," said Liza, "and I've come to get you!"

"No! No!" said Louise, "What have I done?"

"You have sipped of the papaya. It's forbidden. You'll be punished."

"Please don't punish me, sir. I only took one sip, a very little sip, to please Eliza."

"Excuses. Excuses. I do not accept excuses."

At this point I pushed open the screen door, then closed it quietly behind me, holding onto the spring to keep the thing from squeaking. Then I crept up to the edge of the porch, straightened my tiara and bent my knees for the take-off.

"Here I come, Louise!" I called out in mid-air. Then I landed in a heap of tulle beside her.

"Who are you, lovely lady?" Louise asked, as she stuck one skinny arm out, pale white as a bone, to help me up.

"I am the Good Fairy," I said and raised my coat hanger wand with one hand, and brushed my sister's dress off with the other. "I have come to save you. But not quite yet."

"Thank you, Good Fairy," said Louise in that goody-goody voice of hers. "Please don't leave me. Promise you won't leave me."

And I didn't. I can say that much for myself. I stood right beside her while Liza led us down the alley to the Dungeon, which was on the next block. We were going to use my basement.

When we got to my backyard there was Caroline Ruth-erfoord, a twelve-year-old who lives next door to me. She was sitting on my swing set.

"Who's that?" Louise whispered.

"The Devil's helper," I said, "and you mustn't trust her."

And then all four of us walked down the cement steps into my basement. It was cold down in the basement. And dark, of course. With the sneezy smell of coal dust all around us.

I felt around in the air above me till I found the light cord. And then I jerked it on. And the light bulb, for a minute, kept swinging back and forth, making shadows rise and fall along the basement walls.

I made Louise let go of my arm, so I could have a conference with Liza. You see, we hadn't planned the game beyond this point, but now that Caroline was with us, we didn't want to stop. It wasn't very often we could show her anything. So we decided we would make Louise climb up through the crawl space to the front part of the house.

At my house what we have is only half a basement, really. The other half is crawl space, three feet high, between the ground and the house. I had tried to climb through once, myself, but it was dark and dirty and I only went halfway. Polka Dot, my cat, used to go up in the crawl space all the time. Sometimes I'd find her sitting at the grill, way down at the other end. I'd see her two green eyes looking out at the street.

Liza walked up to Louise and pointed to the crawl space. "There's the Dungeon. Up there. You must crawl into the Dungeon."

"How far?" Louise asked, standing very still and holding tight onto a pipe beside the furnace.

"To the end!" I said. "To that little metal grill with the daylight shining through it."

Liza rattled her rake. "*Up* into the Dungeon!"

"We'd better take her dress off first." I said because I knew we'd get in trouble if Louise got soot on her purple party dress. So we took the dress off. And her white socks and her shoes.

"Help me, Good Fairy," Louise whispered in my ear while I was peeling off her sock, "Don't let them make me do it. Please, Good Fairy. I am frightened of the dark!"

I didn't listen to her, though. I just kept yanking at her sock. The scareder Louise got the more excited I got. All of a sudden, I was something more important than myself. I could tell that Caroline thought so, too, standing there so quiet, watching me.

I could have saved Louise. I know it. Anytime I wanted. All I had to do was wave my wand and say "Stop!" But don't you see? Once I did that, the whole game would be over. It would pop, like a balloon. And then I would be nothing but myself, again. Standing in my basement.

So, when I had finished taking off the socks, I stepped back and watched while Liza pushed Louise forward with the rake.

"Watch out for the nails up there," I said. "Watch out for the rusty nails." I could see Louise's bony shoulders shaking through the lace-trimmed petticoat.

"*Up* into the Dungeon," Liza said. And she rattled her rake.

"Help me! Help me!" Louise sobbed these long dramatic movie star sobs, while Liza marched her over to the brick wall she was going to have to climb to reach the crawl space. "Please," Louise said. "Won't *somebody* help me?"

I could hear some thunder rumbling, somewhere off behind the house. And Louise rolled her eyes toward it, and then over at me, for one last look at me which I can't get off my mind.

After that, she stepped up on the silver trunk that we keep right beside the crawl space, covered with soot, like everything down there, and I remember how her bare feet left three prints on top of it.

"Come on, now," said Liza. "Get on up into the Dungeon."

"The Dungeon. The Dungeon," I said. "Up into the Dungeon."

Louise put her hands on the shelf of the wall above her and began to pull herself up. Liza jumped up on the trunk then and gave Louise a boost up from behind.

I saw Louise's knee scrape on the rough bricks of the wall, and begin to bleed a little. But she didn't notice it, she just kept pulling with her arms till she got her whole body up into the crawl space.

Then she waited a minute. Right there at the edge huddled on all fours, like a little animal, in nothing but her cotton petticoat. She had stopped sobbing now and she was looking down at us.

"Go on *in!*" I said.

"To the grill," Liza said. And she raised her rake again.

Louise turned her head around and started crawling very slowly, back into the blackness.

I kept my eyes on her until the whiteness of the petticoat was swallowed up completely by the dark.

"Watch out for the nails!" Liza shouted after her.

Then I got a new idea. "And watch out for the *snakes!*"

Liza went with Caroline around to the front yard, to wait for Louise to come through to the grill. And I stayed there in the basement to make sure she didn't turn around.

So I stepped up on the silver trunk and looked, deep as I could, into the crawl space. But all I saw was darkness, and way down at the end tiny specks of daylight coming through the grill.

The thundering had stopped.

And then I heard some raindrops hitting on the bricks beside the basement window.

The door at the top of the basement steps swung open and Liza came running down. Her yellow hair was soaking wet.

She had taken off her cape and the mustache and looked like herself again.

"Louise hasn't come through!" she said. "Do you think she's hurt herself?"

I felt a thud in my chest, just like a foot had stepped on it. What had we done to Louise?

I scrambled up into the crawl space, bridesmaid's dress and all, and started feeling for her. But she wasn't near the edge.

"Get the flashlight. Quick!" I yelled down to Liza. "On the shelf. Over there, beside the furnace."

Liza handed up the flashlight. And I clicked it on, and started crawling forward, deep into the darkness, with this shaky beam of light that ended in a yellow dot. First the dot landed on an old tin can. Then a Coca-Cola bottle. Then it jumped along the rough brick foundations of the house.

All of a sudden, two bright yellow eyes jumped out of the darkness. I shined the light toward them. And there was Polka Dot, my cat. I hadn't seen her all day long. She was rubbing her black back, up and down, on something white. Against somebody's leg!

I shifted the light over. And there I saw Louise sitting cross-legged on the ground, smiling a funny little smile and staring straight ahead.

"Here I am, Louise," I said in my fairy-tale voice. "I have come to save you now. Our game is finished."

Louise didn't say a word. In fact she didn't even move, so I crawled over and took hold of her hand. Then I pulled her out beside me, like a dog on a leash. And she didn't seem to mind that. She didn't mind a thing. I don't even think she knew who I was.

Liza was waiting at the silver trunk for us. "See," Liza said, as she helped Louise down. "It was just me all along. There wasn't any Devil. I'm sorry if I scared you."

Louise didn't answer Liza.

We led her over to the basin where Molly does the laundry and washed the soot off of her face and off her arms and legs. We couldn't do much with the petticoat, so we slid her dress on over it. And got the socks and shoes on. And she looked as good as new.

Only she didn't talk, of course. She just kept smiling that funny little smile, like she was drunk.

Liza stayed there with Louise while I ran upstairs and changed back to my shorts. Then we took her out the back way so we wouldn't run into my mother.

The rain had stopped. The street was wet, with car tires swishing on it. And the air was cool and clean.

When we got up to the big house, Liza rang the bell. And

this time, it was the maid who came to the door. The big fat one who used to chase us from the yard.

"Here's Louise," Liza said. "She's finished playing with us."

What Ever Happened to Agnes Mason?

"Eye-yah-yah *yike* us. No-bo-dy *like* us. We are the girls from Saint May-ree's. Always a-winninn'. Always a-grinnin'. Always a-feeling' fine…"

While the varsity sang, Miss Richie sat very still on the front seat of the bus, cradling a box of brand new hockey balls. She was a lean, flat-chested woman in her late twenties, with a face already leathered by the winds of the playing fields. This afternoon she wore a white blazer, a brown golf skirt, and a silver whistle which, with the lurching of the bus, bounced on and off her breast-bone, as if off a backboard. Her thin socks were rolled down over her black hockey shoes, exposing chilblains that proclaimed an Englishwoman.

Miss Ritchie was the only adult traveling with the St. Mary's varsity (except for the bus driver, who, turtle-like, had drawn his head so far down into his shoulders one could hardly count him). She was sitting sideways on the front seat with her feet firmly planted in the aisle, as she watched the swaying rows of adolescent girls in identical white blouses, black tunics, and black cotton stockings.

Suddenly, Miss Ritchie squinted. Then cupped her hand at her mouth and shouted, "Mason! Why aren't you singing?"

While her teammates rocked with song, Agnes Mason had not moved a muscle. She merely stared out the window, her long legs intertwined as bonelessly as two pipe cleaners, her pale blue eyes as vacant as swimming pools in November.

"Did you hear me, Mason?"

Muffie Rucker, the pudgy girl sitting next to Agnes stuck an elbow in her ribs, and Agnes turned from the window then, languidly, with one shaggy eyebrow unmistakably arched, "Did someone call me?"

"Yes, I did," said Miss Ritchie in the nasal tones of Lancashire. "I should like to ask a favor of you. Would you bring that mind of yours back to earth for the next two hours? That is all I ask. For just two hours. Until we have won the South Shore trophy. After that, you may let it rise up into orbit once again. And we'll see that you get back on the bus."

Everybody laughed, a hearty, all-pals-together laugh. Even Muffie Rucker, Agnes's roommate, laughed, though as she did so, her eyes shuttled nervously from Agnes's face to Miss Ritchie's to Agnes's again.

"Is that agreeable, Mason?"

"Yes, ma'am," Agnes said softly.

"Very well. And remember that a little team spirit never

hurts a player. Am I right, girls?"

"Is she right?" cried Dodie Whitlock, the captain of the team, as her arm shot above her head, her forefinger slashed the air, and another song began: "Team spirit. Team spirit. We've all got team spirit. And from our team spirit our victory will grow."

Under the hawk-like gaze of Miss Ritchie, Agnes began to sing, too. But she hated herself for doing so, for letting everybody know that deep down she was a lily-livered chicken. When it came to a showdown, you could count on her to swallow her pride and say, "Yes, ma'am." Hadn't she said it that very morning to the teacher who criticized the way she ate her oranges? And to the monitor in study hall who accused her of sleeping on her history book? Agnes loathed herself for every "Yes, ma'am" she had spoken that day, for in her heart she knew that it was not what Scarlett O'Hara would have said.

Exactly eighteen days ago today, Agnes had seen the movie that had changed her life. The funny thing was, she hadn't wanted to see it. The history teacher had made her go; she'd made all the boarders go on the grounds that this was an old film classic, rich in American history, which might not be reissued again for many years. So Agnes had gone expecting the worst — and the movie had changed her life. She had walked into that theater a giggling adolescent. Four hours later, she had emerged a woman.

Her values were totally different now. For example, it no longer seemed important that she had the longest legs at St. Mary's, that year after year, though she was essentially uncoordinated, she made the varsity as wing in the hockey season, guard in the basketball season, and high jumper in the spring. It was far more important that she had bristly black lashes and that when she wore a certain turquoise scarf that belonged to Muffie Rucker, one could almost say her eyes were green.

Apparently, none of her friends had experienced this awakening. Through they wept with each new tragedy that was heaped upon Scarlett, as soon as they left the theater they forgot her. So Agnes was left to bear the agony alone, with no one to comfort her but Muffie Rucker, who was as sympathetic as a lap dog and just about as smart.

Every night after lights-out, Agnes would sneak into her closet with a flashlight and a heavy volume bound in Confederate gray. Then she would creep back into bed, to act out scenes with her pillow, which was frequently cast as Rhett Butler.

Agnes had begun to live for these nights, because the days were getting worse and worse. Groggy from lack of sleep, dazzled by antebellum glories, she seemed to stumble from one crisis to another, attracting demerits as a dog attracts fleas. Within the space of a single hour, she might forget to polish her oxfords, leave her toothpaste in the john, and plop into her seat before grace had been said. This week she, who was accustomed to straight As in citizenship, had been sent to the headmistress for dozing in algebra class.

If things were bad in her classes, they were much worse in gym. Whenever a regular teacher jumped on her, her classmates rallied around her after class with secret signals of approval even open condolences. But when Miss Ritchie jumped on her, Agnes was alone. Her former friends smoldered with disapproval. "Nobody bucks the coach. Don't you know she's one of us? Where is your team spirit anyway?"

The answer was, of course, that it was gone with the you-know-what. But even Agnes dared not admit this yet. Instead she drove herself up and down the hockey field in a breathless, thoughtless effort to endure through the season. Once the winter sports began, she had decided to switch from basketball to swimming where there was much less pressure to win, and she could work in some badly needed practice on the breaststroke.

All the way to Southport High School, Agnes mouthed the words to school songs and meditated on her problems. They would kill her if she goofed today, not just Miss Ritchie, but the whole bus-load of so-called friends. They would turn on her as surely as a pack of wolves will turn on the one that's down. It was the biggest game of the year, the South Shore Finals. They would simply pulverize her if she made them lose it. As long as she could keep her mind on the game, she knew she would be all right. It all would be over in two hours. Surely, she could concentrate on anything for just two hours.

Agnes had worked herself into a mood that one might almost call aggressive when, a few blocks short of its destination, the bus passed a movie theater displaying a life-size poster of Clark Gable crushing Vivien Leigh's lips to his, while red and yellow flames devoured Atlanta. When she caught sight of that poster, her determination melted like butter in an oven. Desperately she tried to pat it back into shape, repeating softly to herself. "This is probably my very last hockey game, ever."

"There's Southport High!" the center forward shouted as two taffy-colored towers emerged from the trees ahead.

"OK, team," called the captain, with her arm in the air again. "Let's go in with 'Eye-yah-yah-yike us.' Good and loud!"

A chilly wind was raising goose pimples on Agnes's bare arms as she held her stick against the fifty-yard line and waited for the opening bully. She hated this part of the game — especially when they were playing a public high school, where the girls were allowed to wear lipstick, and tight belts, and socks that showed their legs off. There were always wise guys in the grandstands making fun of St. Mary's, especially their long black hockey stockings. This afternoon she heard one boy say, "They look like Creepy Crawlers. Hey, there, spider legs!"

It was the bane of being a wing; you had to stand next to the grandstands for one entire half. Once the playing started, it wasn't so bad, because St. Mary's usually creamed their opponents, who failed to look so sexy when they were sweating and puffing and the score was ten to nothing. Then the grandstands would simmer down to a respectful silence — unless, oh Lord, unless the referee called a wing bully before Agnes had switched to the far side of the field.

At last, the center forwards bullied: "Ground, sticks, ground, sticks, ground, sticks, *smash*" to the Southport center half, who sent a fast pass out to the alley.

Agnes intercepted and began to dribble toward the goal, her long black legs spinning up the alley like the spokes of one great wheel. With a flick of her stick, she scooped the ball over the Southport half-back's stick till there was nothing but a clear green field between herself and the goalie.

When she reached the circle, Agnes drew her stick back, as if preparing for a drive, then deftly flicked the ball to the inner, who slammed the ball into the cage for the first goal.

The whistle blew. The three St. Mary's substitutes cheered. And Agnes Mason trotted back to the fifty-yard line, her eyes cast modestly on the grass-blades at her feet, while her heart was pounding a song of triumph in her ears.

The center forwards bullied again. This time, Southport kept the ball, working it slowly down the far side of the field.

In the monotonous gray sky above her, the pale November sun flickered like a fading flashlight bulb. The air was raw and cold and tore at Agnes's throat. She began to stomp her feet to keep her toes from going numb.

Southport got their goal, finally, and the grandstands went wild. While their sassy little cheerleaders, with bare legs and bobby socks and bright red pleated skirts turned cartwheels on the grass.

The score was one to one. This Southport team was good. Not showy, but stubborn. They kept pushing, inch by inch, till they got the ball inside the goal again. St. Mary's was behind now. Agnes glanced across the field to see Miss Ritchie's reaction, but Miss Ritchie's face was a pale, grim mask.

Within five minutes, the St. Mary's center half made a goal and brought the score back to a tie. By the time the ball came out to Agnes again, she was dizzy with fatigue. Somehow she forced her legs to run a little farther, and she could feel her garters straining and contracting on her thighs. The Southport halfback met her at the ball. Both girls pushed their sticks against it till it popped across the sideline.

"Wing bully!" called the referee, and Agnes felt her stomach turn a perfect somersault. Of all possible disasters, this was the supreme one, yet she had no choice but to line up with her back to the grandstands and endure what would inevitably follow.

The problem was, briefly, that the manufacturers made the hockey stockings just so long and the bloomers just so long, and on Agnes's legs there was unavoidably a gap between them — three inches of pink skin, edged with black, and striped with garters. As a rule, this gap was hidden by her tunic but when she leaned over to bully, a roar of pure delight would erupt from the crowd.

Today was no exception. First there was an isolated explosion of surprise. Then a roar of laughter mushroomed from the grandstands and rained on Agnes's bent back. As soon as she could pass the ball, she did so, and streaked down the field, away from the stands

The half-time break was over much too soon. Within five minutes, Agnes was gasping for breath again. Still, she forced her legs to keep on pumping up the field and down the field. The next time a long pass came out to her alley, she heard a crunching of leaves in the open field beside her, and saw a wire-haired terrier racing her for the ball. He won the race with little difficulty, snatched the ball in his teeth, and bounded playfully across the neighboring field.

"I'll get it," Agnes shouted as she dropped her stick and ran after the dog. He was trotting now, his short, blunt tail erect with pride in his achievement. Agnes trotted, too, at first. Then she broke into a run. The dog began to run, too.

When he reached the road in front of Southport High, the dog let Agnes catch up with him. But as soon as she lunged for his collar, he sprang away again and galloped gaily down the block, across the street, around the corner.

Agnes followed wearily. She could have kicked herself for offering to catch the stupid dog. After all, Miss Ritchie had a dozen extra hockey balls. But now that she had committed herself in public, she felt she had to follow through.

So just as the dog had done, Agnes crossed the street and turned the corner. When she did so, she stepped into an entirely different world. It was a quiet residential street, with bright gold maple trees lining the sidewalks. Halfway down the block, a man was burning leaves, and the smell reminded Agnes of autumns in Fredericksburg before her mother got divorced and sent her off to boarding school.

As she walked along, she watched the smoke from the burning leaves drift lazily across the road, fluttering like a transparent scarf and distorting everything that lay beyond it. The terrier was sitting perfectly still in the middle of the road — his head cocked to one side with the white ball in his mouth — yet his body seemed to undulate like an image under water.

Suddenly Agnes felt a delicious sense of freedom. Not the frantic seizure of freedom she had felt the time the Upper School went to the opera and the chaperone got locked in the john. This was something deeper, something more serene.

Her legs, which had been so heavy a few minutes before, now seemed to lift themselves, carrying her down the street as effortlessly as the wind carried the smoke. When she reached the dog, he wagged his tail and obligingly dropped the ball into her hand.

For a moment Agnes studied the hockey ball, the poor, inanimate victim of a senseless game. Less than an hour ago it had been in Miss Ritchie's cardboard box, gleaming white and smooth as marble. Now it was crisscrossed with grass stains and dented from a hundred blows. Among the scars Agnes could distinguish several rows of tiny teeth marks.

She turned the ball in her hand once, then relaxed her fingers and let it slide down to the road, where it bounced once and rolled into the gutter. Neither Agnes nor the dog gave it another thought. Agnes began to walk on toward the traffic light that shimmered in the distance, while the dog galloped off to meet a collie. She had not really made a decision, Agnes realized later. She had simply given in to the whim that drew her down the road.

It was a beautiful walk. The trees were burning amber, red, and gold around her, forming a tunnel of fire that led to the unknown. Every step revealed some unexpected pleasure — a squirrel broad-jumping in the branches above her, a birdhouse built like a Swiss chalet, a hopscotch game scrawled in pale-blue chalk across the sidewalk.

She didn't notice the movie theater till she was standing face to face with a poster of Clark Gable. It was as if he had stepped out on the sidewalk to say "Hello." She stared back at him a minute, then began to walk around behind the ticket booth, studying the glossy photographs that were posted there. All of a sudden, the center doors opened, and the intermission crowd spilled out into the street.

When the same crowd drifted back into the theater, it included a pair of long, black spider legs. And as the house lights dimmed and the stereo system struck up the Tara theme, Agnes settled down into her seat with the sigh of a glutton confronting a smorgasbord.

They found her just as Melanie was losing her baby. An usher came down the aisle, raking the rows with his flashlight beam until it shone on a pair of intricately intertwined legs in black stockings.

Miss Ritchie and Muffie Rucker were waiting in the lobby. Miss Ritchie began to scream as soon as she saw Agnes. "Do you realize what you've done, Agnes Mason? You've caused needless trouble to the Southport police. You've disgraced Saint Mary's School. You've endangered your team's standing…"

The voice that welled up in response from Agnes's throat was a strong contralto, which Muffie Rucker could swear she had never heard before. It cut right through Miss Ritchie's querulous soprano. "Great balls of fire." Agnes said. "Who gives a damn?"

This was the last thing Agnes said until she got back to St. Mary's. There was no need to say more. She had silenced Miss Ritchie. All the way home in the taxi, which they had to take because the bus had gone ahead, Miss Ritchie watched her as warily as she would have watched a bobcat temporarily placed in her charge. Muffie Rucker watched her, too, but with idolatry, not fear, for Agnes Mason had won a disciple with a single sentence.

When they reached the school, Agnes was taken directly to the Infirmary where she spent the next three days reading the heavy gray volume Muffie Rucker smuggled in with her pajamas.

The psychiatrist called it growing pains, recommended rest, and billed the school for fifty dollars. But down in the teachers' smoking room, Miss Ritchie announced that it was something far more serious than that. Wasn't there proof enough in the fact that the child still hadn't asked who won the game?

The Fence

She's almost a landmark on Lafayette Street — the fragile old lady shouldering into the mile that separates St. Luke's Church from her apartment. She always wears a hat. In summer, it's black straw. In winter it's black felt, or on Sundays, mink to celebrate the upswing in her fortunes when the water rights, attached to her grandfather's ruined iron works, were sold.

This summer evening she is walking back from her apartment to the church, for a congregational meeting. She is custodian of the church. The vestry created the job in the Depression to keep her and her mother and her sisters from starving.

Now she will not give it up.

Her name, Lulee Cary Andrews, is printed on the program for the Sunday morning service, and her face — with its white hair and coal black eyebrows — on the minds of several thousand tourists to whom she has explained the history of St. Luke's.

Generally, she trumpets the names and dates from her lips, intermittently at first, so that each one seems a single entity, like the first raindrop. Then almost imperceptibly, there is a quickening of tempo; names and dates, dates and names begin to follow faster, rising to a magnificent crescendo, after which, with a jerk of the head that is almost casual, she indicates the pew where Lee worshiped.

Tonight the congregation of St. Luke's has been called together to vote on a proposed addition to the church building. The architect's model sits waiting for inspection in the transept, showing the original church with the new wing that will be wedged into the hill beside it, an ingenious plan combining a Sunday school and meeting room on the street level with a commercial garage underneath.

And that part is perfectly all right with Lulee. She has never been, like so many of her friends, categorically opposed to progress. In fact, she was intending to support the vestry's plan completely until this afternoon, when she woke up to the fact that the vestry had gone too far.

*****

The chimes had just finished tolling three o'clock when two young men from the architect's office arrived with the model. Lulee held the door open for them, and the young men shuffled in, with tiny drops of perspiration trailing down their temples, as they bore the future St. Luke's into the present one, the first man backing blindly through the doorway, the second now and then whispering a warning as the miniature steeple careened toward the doorsill.

Finally, they set the model down on the card table Lulee had set up in the transept and she signed a receipt for it, forcing the pencil to glide in generous loops until it had completed the familiar signature. "Lulee C. L. Andrews, Custodian."

After the young men left, she sat down on the front pew to study the model. She sensed that there was something wrong with it. Not in the strident whiteness of the tiny buildings. She discounted that, knowing that soon enough the soot from the city would soften it to gray. Not in the artificial trees, stuck down like lollipops at even intervals in the plaster frosting to assure the donor of the site, Margaret Taylor Hughes, that the condition of her gift had not been forgotten: "that any building on the site be recessed from the sidewalk twenty-five feet and no less than four magnolia trees and two willow oaks be planted before it."

No, there was something wrong with the original church.

Lulee strained forward in the pew, her back bending till her eyes were level with the tiny steps leading to the tiny portico. Tiny, naked steps, she thought, and then she realized what was wrong.

The iron fence was gone.

Her back snapped straight and she sat there motionless, except for the rapid rise and fall of her chest and the trembling of the twisted fingers in her lap.

She knew it was deliberate. During the first seconds of the shock she dismissed the soothing voice that said, "Maybe they just forgot to put it on the model. That don't mean they plan to tear it down." Because she knew the young minister, Mr. Swift, and those smooth-talking business men on the vestry well enough to know that the fact that the fence was never mentioned in her presence was evidence that this was a surreptitious act.

The architect had included the fence along the side of the

church in his model. Why then, not in front of the steps? They knew she would object to any tampering with the original church. When they brought up a proposal to poke holes in the ceiling for indirect lighting, she had made the junior warden leave the vestry room and walk into the church with her and look at what they were about to ruin — plasterwork that architects from all over the country came to see. She stopped them then; so this time they had worked behind her back. "And you deserve it," she could hear her sister saying, as if she were alive today. "If you're gonna play with fire, and write up its minutes, and take up for its doings, then when you get burnt yourself, you will deserve it."

In Lulee's tidy mind — where thoughts were generally stored like folded linen on designated shelves — protests, accusations, and arguments were exploding now, as if a crate of firecrackers had been accidentally ignited. So she sat very still, until the last explosion. Then out of the debris she began to sort the facts that were important.

It was wrong to tear the fence down; she must not let them do it. The muscles in her body responded to this fact as they would have responded to a physical fact — a door to be opened, a suitcase to be lifted.

That fence was a work of art, designed by the original architect to go with the Greek Revival church. She was always pointing out to people how its delicate acanthus leaves matched the ones in plaster on the ceiling inside.

The fence was useful, too. For more than a century it had been protecting St. Luke's from downtown traffic. You could see it in the Mathew Brady photographs and all those people back then, including President Davis and General Lee, must have passed through its gates a hundred times at least. Which was another reason that the fence should be preserved. As a memorial to great men. Lord knows, there had been precious few passing through it since.

But Lulee knew it would be risky to use this argument. She'd noticed more and more that young people do not like to be reminded of the past. Particularly Richmond's past and this church's part in it.

As she sat there on the front pew, absolutely still, with these thoughts churning in her mind, Lulee wondered how she was ever going to put them into words. Because she had decided she would have to speak tonight. And it is what she's going to say, choosing the words that she will use, that is absorbing her attention now, as she walks back to the church from her apartment, with a slapdash supper undigested in her stomach.

Her lips are moving silently, as she strings words into ropes that she will try to fling across the generations. She is so occupied with words that she does not even look up when she reaches the church and the iron fence she will be fighting for tonight. Her hand reaches out mechanically and swings the gate back on its hinges.

"Hey, Aunt Lulee!" It's her nephew Cary calling from the far side of the portico. She climbs the steps diagonally to say hello to him, though she knows she has his vote already. You can always count on Cary to vote against change. Any change. Tonight he will be voting not just against the idea of tearing down the fence but against the whole notion of putting up a wing. On the very first count, the vestry had numbered Cary Andrews among its unpersuadable opponents.

She can also count on the votes of the members of the Historic Richmond League and the Association for the Preservation of Antiquities. But in this day and age those votes are not enough. She has heard the vestry analyze the membership; it is a matter of mathematical fact that the activists, the unconditional supporters of Mr. Swift and the senior warden, Conway Taylor, have a comfortable margin. To save the fence tonight, she'll have to win some votes from them.

Mr. Swift starts off the meeting with a prayer, asking the Lord for the wisdom to see the special needs of a downtown church, the courage to undertake a bold plan for its survival, and the patience to withhold small personal objections to the architect's model in the interest of a greater good, the future of God's work in this parish.

Afterwards, he sits down in the choir stalls, while Conway Taylor, chairman of the board of the Commonwealth Bank and senior warden of the church, takes over the meeting.

Lulee watches Conway's polished black shoes mount the marble steps to the chancel, then pause and turn to face the congregation. His miracle-fabric suit shows no sign of the heat that has fallen on the city like a sour wash rag: his forehead has no sheen of perspiration on it, as if the heat, too, is aware of his unspoken economic power and does not want to tangle with him.

He begins by explaining the plan to finance the new building with a thirty-year mortgage defrayed by the income from the garage.

Lulee is sitting with her nephew in the Andrews pew, five rows from the front, on the gospel side. She is waiting for a pause from Conway Taylor, a chance to interrupt him and speak out to the crowd. And she can feel her heart pounding in her rib-cage — the boom, boom, booms traveling along her veins up to her neck and then into her eardrums, where, reproduced again, they threaten to drown out the sound of Conway Taylor's words.

When she finally does hear the call, it is not, as she expects, a call for comment, but a quick, perfunctory nod in the direction of the by-laws: "If there are no objections to the design, as presented in this model, we will go on to consider..."

The boom, boom, booms in her ears are so loud now that she has to shout above them. Her mouth falls open and her lungs inhale and she says "Wait!"

Right away the pounding stops, and she realizes she has spoken too loud.

"What is it, Miss Lulee?"

Conway Taylor asks in a voice so subdued it seems to reprimand her for shouting in the church.

Now everyone is looking at her. She can feel the rows and rows of faces behind her burning into her back and can see the four rows of them in front of her twisting on their necks. And for a second she seems to have no muscles in her legs. As she stares in horror at her lifeless knees, they respond without warning, thrusting her small body up against the pew in front, so that she has to grab hold of it to keep from falling over it.

She takes a deep breath, then, and forces out the statement that is lodged in her larynx, expels it with a sudden gust of air, as she has seen her great-nephew expel a dried pea from a hollow tube.

"About the fence," she says, pronouncing the "about" somewhere between "a boat" and "a boot" as Virginians generally do. "I don't think you ought to tear down the fence."

"We don't' plan to tear down the fence, Miss Lulee," Conway Taylor says. "Only that portion of the fence that is in front of the steps. The architect believes, and the vestry agrees, that it makes the church seem inaccessible."

"Oh, please don't tear it down!" She hears her voice pleading; she won't win votes by pleading. So she reaches back into the closet of her mind, where she has stored so many strings of words and seizes the first one she comes upon.

"That fence is an attraction for the tourists. Just last week a man from Michigan came in here to see St. Luke's and he said, 'Where'd you get that fence?' And I said it had been here since the church was built in 1845. And he said 'Hang onto that fence. You don't see many churches with a fence like that one.' "

As she mouthed the words, she looks around at the faces that are turned toward her. Open, empty faces, but at least open faces — not locked up for the day behind a handsome mask like Mr. Swift's or Conway Taylor's.

"That's exactly what he said," she continues, releasing one hand from the walnut rail and half-turning toward the rows of faces behind her. "It's part of the original church and we ought to hang on to it, don't you know? No tellin' what it would cost us, if we set about to buy it.

"And we need that fence there for protection. A church that's in the middle of the city needs something to discourage drunks from sleeping on the steps. The gates aren't ever locked. Anyone who wants to come into the church, because it is a church, can always do that. But the fence is out there to discourage the others."

What are all those faces thinking? That she's curious and quaint? She doesn't mind that when she's taking people on the tour. But it's not what she needs now.

Yet what else can she say? That they mustn't violate the magic circle? If she starts that kind of talk, they'll think she's crazy. Unless they, too, have stood across the street on a winter afternoon and seen the pale gray spire merge into the sky, while the little fence below it bristles like a porcupine, its iron needles fending off invaders — convoys of trucks, battalions of shoppers. Lord, if she starts to talk like that, they'll think she's lost her mind.

Lulee takes a deep breath and flings out one last string of words.

"That fence is historic. It is part of Richmond's past. You can see it there in all the old engravings, because it's been here from the start, don't you know? And it was here during the War, when General Lee and all those people came here to church."

By accident, she's done it — mentioned the name that means so much to her and nothing to these young people except some vague, unwanted link to the days of slavery. And by doing so, she's forfeited their votes.

Lulee's knees collapse, and she sits down.

Sure enough, an arm shoots up across the aisle. It belongs to the young surgeon with the Van Dyke beard; the youngest member of the vestry

"Surely you don't mean to say that we have to keep that fence just because General Lee may have touched it. If you want to know the truth, I'm getting just a wee bit tired of the General and his crowd. It never ceases to amaze me how much time and energy, to say nothing of money, is wasted in this town on building and preserving monuments to losers."

Margaret Taylor Hughes, Conway Taylor's sister, and the donor of the building site murmurs, "That's not fair," while Sarah Winston Smith, founder of the Historic Richmond Guild, leaps to her feet and thunders in a hoarse contralto. "I suggest you read more deeply into history, young man. And re-examine your definition of a loser. Or you may discover that you are one yourself."

A murmur of amusement ripples through the pews. Nearly everybody there has, at one time or another, been a victim of Sarah Winston Smith's tart tongue.

The young doctor is blushing, as he prepares to answer.

But before he has a chance, Conway Taylor intervenes.

"We cannot take the time tonight to go into each individual's objections to details in the plan..." The words flow from his lips, as smoothly as syrup from a silver pitcher: "...The Women's Auxiliary believes we need a second oven in the kitchen. The Sunday school superintendent prefers green blackboards. Of course, your vestry wants to hear all of these suggestions at the end of this meeting. I will see that they are given full consideration. But now, if we want to get home before midnight, I suggest that someone make a motion that we consider only the primary question: Shall we authorize the contractor to begin construction of the new wing? Or shall we abandon this plan for expansion?"

"I so move," says a voice from the back of the church.

"Second."

"It has been moved and seconded..." Just like that, slowly and smoothly and without interruption, the attention of the congregation is drawn away from the fence as Lulee has seen a wave sucked from the shore by the outgoing tide.

"It has been moved and seconded that we confine this evening's discussion to the primary question..."

Suddenly, across the aisle and two rows up. Lulee sees a slender arm with thick, gold bracelets on it, waving. It is Margaret Taylor Hughes's arm. Conway Taylor sees it, too, and says, "Yes, Margaret?"

"I want to go on record." Mrs Hughes stands up and turns to face the center aisle. She is a handsome woman in her early sixties with her gray hair drawn back from her temples in a loose French knot. The vestry assumed that Mrs. Hughes's vote would be controlled by her brother, Conway Taylor. Yet here she is standing up and saying in a voice that is shaking with emotion. "I want to go on record in support of Miss Lulee. I see no reason to tear down any part of that fence. In fact, if I had known that this new wing would lead to arbitrary changes in the church itself, I would not have given you the land for it."

She turns then and faces her brother, Conway Taylor, squarely. "I wish to have it put into the record, Conway, that I am ashamed to have my name connected with such meaningless destruction."

As Margaret Taylor Hughes sits down, a hush falls over the entire congregation and they savor the predicament of Conway Taylor, the way a moviegoer savors the silence right before the draw, when the Best Shot in the West has met his equal.

But if they are hoping to see Conway Taylor shoot it out with his sister, they vastly underestimate him. One of the skills responsible for his success in business is a remarkable tact which can convert a small defeat into a larger victory. He has learned never to linger over a defeat, but simply to plow it under, until it is indistinguishable from the substance of success.

Without even changing the tone of his voice, he says, "The fence or lack of fence is a minor matter, really. Since there seems to be strong feeling for it. I shall instruct the architect to leave the fence intact. Now, if I may return to the motion on the floor..."

So it's over. Just like that. Lulee's words have reached somebody after all. For one split second, across a generation, two minds have connected. A sister has stood up to her brother.

And the fence has been saved.

After the new wing is voted in, by a majority more generous than the vestry anticipated, the meeting is adjourned.

Lulee catches a ride home to her apartment with her nephew, Cary. But she does not hear what he is saying to her in the car. Her mind is still too full of echoes from her sudden victory; her heart, too busy pounding a noisy song of triumph in her ears.

Later, though, as she reaches out to switch off the lamp beside her bed, the noises stop. And in the sudden silence, she realizes that not a word she spoke tonight got through to that young surgeon or his friends. And in the long run, they — not Margaret Taylor or her brother Conway — will be making the decisions for St. Luke's.

Under the lamp beside her bed, a photograph of her father, posing shyly in his regimental uniform, stares at her with dark, almost accusing eyes.

"All right, Papa, what would you have said to them? You can't imagine how much things have changed."

Now she is remembering another summer evening, more than eighty years ago. A crowd of relatives and friends have gathered on the porch of their house at 4 West Lafayette Street and they are rocking in their chairs and swapping war stories. Her father rises quietly and walks into the house.

She, who is still a little girl then, runs after him and stops him in the hall. "Why do you do that, Papa? Can't you see it hurts their feelings: Why won't you stay with them and talk about the War?"

"Four years were enough for me," he says. "Lulee, let me tell you this much. It was the worst mistake we ever made."

"Forgive us our mistakes." That's what Papa would have said to that young doctor and his friends.

And it's what Christ would have said, too. Does say — in one of those newfangled translations of the Prayer Book that she has never liked because they rob the language of its richness. "Forgive us our mistakes, as we forgive those who make mistakes against us."

New words for an old-time cure for shame. And maybe even youth.

Lulee switches off the light and lets her head fall into the feather pillow.

Less than a minute later, she's asleep.

The Gift

As soon as the baby, Rob, wakes up from his nap, Aunt
Maria is going to take the children swimming. Even Laura
who has a cold and can't go into the water. Because the
whole point is to get the children out of Grandma's house,
so Clare's mother and Big Laura can divide up the china in
peace and quiet. All week long they have been saving gas
coupons for the drive to the pool at Natural Bridge.

Clare is waiting now on the front porch swing. Sometimes it seems to her that all she does these days is wait. As
she gives a good hard push against the porch floor boards,
she notices that they are crusted with old paint underneath
the new paint that her grandmother had Joe, the yard man,
put on it the week before she died.

Funny, Clare thinks. How she didn't feel a thing when
her mother told her that Grandma had died. Not a thing
except relief that those sharp blue eyes that always saw

around the corners of a person's conversation were closed now, thank the Lord.

It wasn't just that Grandma was so strict — about manners at the table and no movies on Sunday. The worst thing was the way that she expected you to be so much better than you were. With the bubble gum, for instance. The PX across the street, at Washington & Lee, is the only place left that still has Double Bubble. Gobs and gobs of it. And they don't seem to care how much you buy. So the last time Clare came up to Lexington, she brought enough money to buy up a whole carton, one hundred pieces, to take back home to Richmond where a single piece is worth a comic book, at least, or three steel jacks. But Grandma wouldn't let her buy it. If bubble gum was scarce, she said, Clare was entitled to one piece for each friend. To buy up a whole box would be unpatriotic.

No use arguing with her. It was better just to wait until she died. Even now Clare feels a nip of fear at the bottom of her stomach as she thinks about the carton sitting at this very minute at the bottom of her suitcase, for there is an outside chance that Grandma was right. Can one tiny act of treason jinx the war?

Of course not, Clare tells herself. How can it possibly hurt, any more than it helped last June on D-Day when Grandma made her walk up to the top of Washington Street and down again to church, with the thin, white summer light draining out behind the mountains to pray for the men involved in the invasion.

When Grandma said for you to pray she really meant it.

No hope of staying on the edges of the thing, bracing your behind against the seat and leaning on the pew in front of you. With those ice pick eyes sticking in your back you had to get down on your knees and turn all the way around — then stare at the greasy, shiny buttons on the seat cushion, while words and spit and bad breath from the grownups in the pew behind you were falling on your head. Clare would have died, she would have absolutely died, if any of her Richmond friends had seen her. Coming home that D-Day night she tried to explain how embarrassing it was to have to pray like that. But Grandma didn't seem to hear her, she didn't seem to care that praying backwards, on your knees, was out of style.

Now all of that is over. Those ice pick eyes are closed, once and for all, and those old unbending bones will soon be as bare as the bones of Lee's horse, Traveller, in Lee Chapel. And there's nobody left who can boss me, Clare thinks.

Suddenly she feels a delicious sense of power at the thought of all that Double Bubble, one hundred pieces, waiting in her suitcase to go back with her to Richmond after her mother and her aunts have divided Grandma's stuff and closed the house.

* * * *

The sun is still shining strong when they get to Natural Bridge. But while they are in swimming a film begins to roll over the mountains. The sky turns white above them, then gradually gray, and the bare, wet skin on Clare's back begins to soak up all the cold. Her fingers, too, she notices are shriveled from the water. "I'm going in to change," she shouts to no one in particular, then grabs a towel and walks back to the locker room.

There is nobody in there, much to her relief. Clare doesn't like to get undressed in front of other people now that she is starting to get bosoms — little chocolate drop bosoms where flat brown wafers used to be. And even worse, last week, when she was stretched out in the bathtub she noticed on those soft, white folds, that made her think of unbaked rolls waiting to be popped into the oven, a long black intimidating hair.

It is coming. She might as well admit it. Her best friend in Richmond, Mercer Spencer, already has it. And on Sunday afternoons when they are walking home from the movies and have to pass an alley, it is she, Clare, who has to step into it first on the theory that if anyone gets raped it had better be Clare since she hasn't got it yet and still can't have a baby.

Pretty soon, though, — Clare is almost certain of it — pretty soon they'll have to stop walking home and take the bus.

She ties her sash into a full, old-fashioned bow like the ones around the necks of Persian cats, then gives it a fluff and walks out to the pool to wait until the others finish swimming.

Laura, the four-year-old who has a cold and cannot go into the water, is playing in a sandbox just beyond the cement border down the long side of the pool. Clare walks over and joins her, taking care not to mash her bow as she crisscrosses her legs and collapses in the sand. She decides to make a sand statue, since she's pretty good at art. She'll make a really good statue to show her Aunt Maria, the youngest and the prettiest of all her aunts.

"Can I use the bucket, Laura?"

Laura nods, to indicate yes. And Clare gets up again, takes four long steps to the edge of the pool, then kneels down gracefully, in case someone is watching, and fills the rusty bucket with chlorine-smelling water.

"Now," she says to Laura as she pours the water on the sand, "When I get it good and wet, I'll make a sand statue."

Generally, Laura does not talk unless she has something to say. She just keeps working on her castle while Clare begins to make a cocker spaniel's head. First, she molds the sand into a firm mound for the face. Then she begins to construct the extension of a nose. She is, in fact, so busy slapping one handful of sand over the other that she does not even look up when she senses someone standing right behind her.

"Clare."

She recognizes her Aunt Maria's voice, a furry voice that purrs from all the places she has been. "Will you be a dear," Aunt Maria says, "and look after Rob while Libby and I go back to the locker room to change?"

Clare cannot speak at first. She is so stunned by the closeness of her gorgeous Aunt Maria in the two-piece bathing suit which may be the only two-piece bathing suit in Rockbridge County. One slim hip is slung out just a bit below the bare, tanned midriff to support the baby — a soft, fat, barely molded lump of flesh in a sailor suit.

"Will you look after Rob?"

"I'd be delighted to," says Clare, surprising herself with a quick and graceful answer when nowadays so many times she finds she cannot think of what to say.

It is the first time in Clare's life that anyone has asked her to look after a baby. "Come on, Rob," she says, holding out her hands as she has seen the baby's sister, Libby, do and hoping that her Aunt Maria will not notice that her fingernails are bitten.

At first the baby simply stares at Clare with enormous blank blue eyes, then suddenly he jerks his chubby arms up, both at once, to indicate permission to be taken.

Aunt Maria laughs. "I think he likes you."

Overjoyed, Clare swings the baby's heavy body across the space between them, bringing it to rest against her own bony shoulder, feeling underneath the smooth starched cotton of the baby's sailor blouse, a cushion of soft flesh across the back. The soles of the baby's shoes are tickling her ribs, but Clare likes the feeling of the fine silk curls and warm face next to hers and the sweet smell of the ointment she has watched her cousin Libby rub into the deep secret creases when she changes his diapers.

After Aunt Maria leaves, Clare sets the baby down gently in the sandbox and begins to show him how to fill the bucket up with sand, then empty it completely and shovelful by shovelful fill it up again. Pretty soon, though, she gets tired of it. Babies, she decides, in the long run are a bore.

"Here," she says to Rob, handing him the metal shovel. "You can do it for yourself now." And with that she turns her attention back to her sand statue which still needs ears, two long curly ears, and eyes which she can carve in later with the shovel.

Clare molds two flat molds of sand for the cocker spaniel's ears and begins to scoop the curls out with her fingers. Suddenly a dimpled hand falls into the statue's nose.

"No, no," she says to Rob, pushing him gently toward the corner of the sandbox opposite the one where Laura is still working on her castle. "You play with the bucket. See?" Clare fills it up for him. "See" And after that she leaves him.

Gently, very gently she packs the statue back together, but the baby crawls right back and demolishes it again.

"Bad boy!" she says. And this time she picks him up and swings him to the far side of the sandbox. "Now stay there. Do you hear? Stay out of my way!"

If doesn't take her long to repair the damage to the statue. Two minutes at the most. And after that, she carves the eyes in with the sharp edge of the shovel which the baby has by this time abandoned in the sand. When she finishes the eyes she starts on the whiskers. How much time goes by? It is impossible to tell. Her mind is bound so tight to the thing that she is making that she will never be able to estimate exactly.

All of a sudden she hears Laura's voice:

"Where's Rob?"

The name, "Rob," plops into the cold gray silence. Then it vanishes like a pebble in a pool of water. Only after it has vanished does its meaning ripple out, in widening circles, on the surface of the silence.

Clare leaps up to her feet and looks around the pool, but the scene appears to be more or less as she left it. The swimming pool, that is, the two-thirds of the pool that she can see from the sandbox, is deserted. And on the other side of it, four ladies are sitting, swaddled in striped beach towels, bunched over a table, playing cards.

"Rob?" Clare shouts the name into the silence again, then listens as its echo bounces off the mountains. The ladies do not look up from their card game, and Clare is glad that they do not. For some reason this seems to be a very private situation.

Her mind is working hard to think up possibilities to block the probability that is too awful to admit. Maybe Rob crawled back to the locker room. Or his mother came and took him away.

"Maybe Aunt Maria came and got him," Clare says, without looking back at Laura, though she can feel Laura's blue eyes boring through her back to the fear that is growing steadily inside.

How long does she stand there thinking without moving? Clare will never know exactly. All she knows that when she can't stand Laura's staring any longer, she gathers up the strings that work her leg muscles and forces her legs to make the four long steps to the edge of the swimming pool.

Then she lets her chin flop down, so that she cannot help but see what is below them. What she knows by now is going to be below them.

Rob. Floating just beneath the surface of the water. The back of his sailor blouse ballooned with air. His brown curls drawn out from his head like unraveled strands of hemp, gently undulating in the water. One shoelace has come untied and the two white ends of it are moving up and down in the gently rocking rhythm of the water.

Almost automatically Clare lifts up one leg and steps over the edge, thinking, as the soles of her shoes hit the surface of the water, how glad she is she hasn't worn her watch.

When she feels her shoes touch bottom she bends her arms and scoops the buoyant body up. Then she begins to wade with it through the chest high water, forcing her body through the pressure of the water while her thin leather soles scrape up the cement slanting toward the shallow end.

The baby's face is upturned in her arms. And she is reading her own future in these soft, silk-surfaced features, immobile as the mountains around them. Since the baby's eyes are closed, she stares at the eyelashes, two feathery brown lines sketched against the smooth white flesh.

"If I get what I deserve, he will be dead," she thinks. "Oh God. Please God. Don't let him be dead." And all the while she keeps on watching the baby's eyelashes for some tiny sign that life has not left him yet. Has not drifted back into the water where her science teacher says it came from a billion years ago.

By now the level of the water has receded to her waist. And the baby in her arms is completely separated from the water except for one thin stream pouring from the back of his water-flattened hair. It is then that, suddenly, the baby's eyes flip open. Like a doll's.

He does not cry. He does not smile. His whole face remains immobile as he looks at her with flat, unjudging eyes. Clare stops walking then, and stands absolutely still to receive whatever is being offered to her, her mind as empty as a cup into which something good is being poured.

But then one of the ladies, the card-playing ladies, brings her back to her senses. They must have heard the splash when Clare jumped into the pool. For they are clustered at the ladder with their bright striped beach towels extended out to her. "Is the baby all right?" one of them asks.

"Yes," Clare says.

And that is all she says for the next half hour.

When she steps into the locker room with water squishing in her shoes, the baby dripping in her arms, Aunt Maria's jaw falls open as if she is about to shout. But she closes it, abruptly, and transferring her anger into action, snatches the baby from Clare's arms. For once in her life, Clare does not try to make excuses. She is, in fact, relieved to be back in a situation where a person gets what she deserves.

By the time they get back to the car, the storm has broken. All the way to Lexington, rain is shifting back and forth in sheets across the road. Uncle Ted, who is a doctor, comes by and examines Rob and finds no trace of water in his lungs. Ordinarily, he says, a baby will try to breathe in the water. But Rob is an exception. He must have caught his breath, in surprise, when he first hit the water. And held it until Clare got him out.

When the others aren't around, Clare asks him how long can a baby hold its breath?

"It depends," her uncle says, "A minute. Maybe two

would be the limit." Clare is practically certain that three minutes elapsed between the time that Laura said, "Where's Rob?" and she forced herself to look into the pool. And no telling how long he was in the water before Laura noticed he was missing.

So she'll have to live with it, this spooky gift from God. But that doesn't mean she has to talk about it. She makes a promise to herself, then and there, that she will never, ever, breathe a word to any living soul about it.

Without answering her uncle, she turns and runs down the hall and bursts through the screen door to the porch. Then remembering too late, she stiffens as the screen door slams like a thunderclap behind her.

She goes over to the swing, plops down on it and tries to swing, but the pressure is too tight inside her chest, as she lets her knees collapse to the porch floor boards. Then she turns around and faces into the swing, bracing her bony elbows on its slats. The words come out like bullets, then, driven by the pressure which has built inside her. "Thank you," she says. Thank you. Thank you, God."

"Clare?"

At the sound of Libby's voice, Clare jumps to her feet and falls back on the swing so that Libby will not catch her praying. Then she gives a good hard push with her feet, so hard that the swing begins to wobble as the screen door opens and Libby steps onto the porch.

"Hi," Libby says, her brown eyes pleading for acceptance as she hangs onto the handle of the door and lets it close quietly behind her. "Can I swing, too?"

"Why not?" Clare says. "It's a free country, isn't it?" And she stops the swing to let her cousin climb aboard it.

The two of them swing there for a moment, listening to the rhythmic clicks as the swing's metal chains switch directions on the ceiling hooks above them. It feels good to let the rain-cooled breeze wash their arms and legs. First the backs, and then the fronts, and then the backs of them again.

"Tell me how it happened." Libby says all of a sudden.

Up till now, Clare realizes, nobody has asked her. And the funny thing is if they had asked her earlier she would have blurted out the truth; she was still so overcome by the gift, or her incredibly good luck, or whatever you finally decided you would call it. But by now she's had some time to pull herself together. Laura is, after all, only four years old. No one will believe her story.

"Well," Clare says, stretching out her skinny legs and rotating her loafers. "After you and your mother went back to the locker room, we stayed in the sandbox. I was playing with Rob, and Laura was working on her sand castle. And she kept on asking me would I please look at it. So finally I did. And when I looked back, Rob was gone."

"Could you see him in the pool?"

"Not from there, I couldn't. I had to walk up to the edge before I saw him."

"Whew!" Libby says. "I would never have thought of that! He would have drowned before I thought of walking over to the edge."

Moron. Don't you understand that you would never have let him fall in the first place? Clare realizes, suddenly, that she is sick to death of Libby and this whole goody-goody family she's been stuck with for a month.

Just then she hears the squeaking wheels of Laura's wagon. Actually it is Grandma's wagon, the same old one that Clare used when she was Laura's age to ride down the steep sidewalk to the foot of Washington Street.

Sure enough, a minute later Laura appears in the gap between the hedges. She stops and turns her head and stares at her cousins, her blue eyes following the motion of the swing.

Fear flashes like a match in the back of Clare's mind. Did Laura hear what she had said to Libby? No, of course, she didn't. Nobody can hear a thing down there on the sidewalk with that stupid wagon making all that racket.

"Hey Laura," Clare shouts. "Did you have a good ride down?"

Laura does not answer. Instead, she turns back to the sidewalk and begins to drag the wagon up the steep slope to the crest of Washington Street, which is still almost half a block away.

The muscles in Laura's small legs knot as she throws her weight and the wagon's weight against the down pull of the hill. As Clare watches this struggle which Laura, who was born here in the mountains, engages in without thinking every day of her life, she feels, all of a sudden, very tired.

Oh Lord, will she be glad when they have closed up Grandma's house and she can go back home where everything is flat.

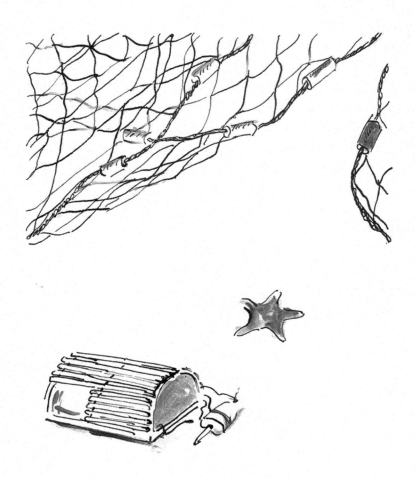

At the Museum

The telephone was ringing, but Eileen Reeves had her girdle only halfway on. Billows of white flesh were foaming at the waistband. She couldn't stop now. No matter who that was.

"Will you get it, Essie?" she shouted toward the hall. "And tell them I'll call back?" She glanced at her watch. "No. Better say I've left. Gone to the airport to meet the Governor. After that, I'll be at the Museum."

At the Museum. I like the sound of that, she thought as she flicked her hip and yanked the girdle higher. After all that I've been through with that mousy little pedant, I still like the sound of that: Mrs. Reeves is — at the Museum. Not…on the golf course. Not…in the garden. But more often than not... at the Museum.

Tenderly she tucked the final fold of flesh into her girdle, then leaned down and yanked her stockings straight. Still damned good-looking legs, she thought, holding one leg out and rotating the foot. And well-turned ankles. That Elcock girl, poor thing, has dreadful ankles. She may have a beautiful mind, but she's got perfectly dreadful ankles. That's probably one reason she went through all that hell to get a Ph.D. She was certain she'd have nothing else to do.

When I think how I've had to fight to keep a little umphf in this exhibition, to make it just a tiny bit different from the 14 other exhibitions of the 14 other museums that signed up for the same set of paintings from Art Express. "I wouldn't do that if I were you." That's what that Elcock creature said about my driftwood. And about my sound effects. And even about my title. My harmless little title: "Winslow Homer, Painter of the Sea." And what was that monstrosity she suggested? "Winslow Homer Retrospective." Now how many people in this county ever heard of "retrospective?" For that matter, how many ever heard of Winslow Homer?

"You've got to make allowances." If I said it to her once, I said it a hundred times. "These people don't have Ph.Ds. They're just small-town people. And half of them have never even laid eyes on the ocean. That's why it's so important that we give them a feeling of the sea," And what did she say then: "Couldn't we leave that to the artist? He was fairly good at it."

Eileen yanked open a dresser drawer, pulled out a lace-encrusted slip and wriggled into it. A partnership, the mayor called it. The perfect partnership to head up Surrey's Art Museum. The partnership of a sorceress and a scholar.

Those were the words he used. A sorceress and a scholar. Why would he call me a sorceress, I wonder? "Because you can work magic." That's what Harry says. "Because you can write checks."

And maybe Harry's right. But did the Mayor really think that I would be content to sit back on my duff and sign all of those checks? And let Jean Elcock nail her 20 little hooks in a neat little row and hang the 20 paintings on them — and call the thing an exhibition? Our premiere exhibition? If the Mayor thought that, he's got another thought coming.

Eileen sat down at the dressing table, leaned up to the mirror, and began to brush her lashes with mascara. Yes sirree, he's got another thought coming. Because I've worked to make my name stand for something in this town. Sophistication, maybe. Creativity. For twelve long years I've slaved as Garden Week Coordinator, Salad Chief at the Lenten Luncheons, Creative Ideas Chairman for the Children's Infirmary Ball. When I could just as well have stuck my nose up in the air and ignored their hicky little projects. Plenty of women with my background would have done just that. But I said to myself when we moved to Surrey, "If you don't like it, change it." And that's been my motto all along.

Sure there have been times when I felt like giving up. Last week, for example, when I got seven phone calls asking what does "Black Tie" mean on the preview invitation. But I kept on fighting. Out of habit mainly. And if I do say so myself, I've built up quite a reputation. And I'll be damned if I will blow it now just to please that prude, Jean Elcock.

A partnership, the Mayor called it. Partnership, hell. It's been a goddam war. But at least, Eileen thought, as she rubbed eyeshadow on her eyelid, at least I think I've won it. If I can just keep her from sticking her nose into that Gallery on her way home from the college. And tossing out my seashells. And messing up my information panels with her timid little *circas*. If I've told her once, I've told her a hundred times, nobody cares about your *circas*. If you think a painting was painted in 1890, go ahead. Be brave. Say 1890. That's what you think now, isn't it? And if 50 years from now somebody digs up a letter, some moth-eaten letter, that proves that it was painted on New Year's Day of 1891, then we'll simply say we made an honest error. Eileen picked up a deodorant pad and slapped it at her armpit. Nobody minds an honest error. Personally, I think an honest error isn't half as offensive as a *circa*.

And there's something else, she thought as she raised the other arm. Something I could not explain to her because she was born without literary feeling. And that is that her *circas* were breaking up the rhythm of my prose. Absolutely no point in explaining that to her. Better to let her go ahead and botch up my copy with her pussyfooting *circas*. It was easy enough to take them out this morning.

Eileen snapped the gold cap back on the eyeshadow stick

and jabbed it in a bud vase that was already sprouting eyebrow pencils, lipstick brushes, and tweezers. But I know Jean Elcock well enough to know that she won't hesitate to put those *circas* back in. If she gets inside that Gallery before the crowd gets there, she'll whip out a ballpoint pen and write them all back in.

Eileen jumped up from the dressing table, pattered over to the Princess telephone beside her bed and dialed the Museum's number. "Hello? May I please speak to Mr. Barnes? ... Mr. Barnes, Eileen Reeves. Just checking to be sure you've got all of my instructions. No one is allowed in the Gallery, right? Till the Governor cuts the ribbon .... That's right. Absolutely no one. Not even Miss Elcock.... Well, of course, the men from Art Express will have to come in. But you won't even see them. Mr. Briggs will bring them in through the back. ... I'd say any minute now. The truck left Louisville at noon. But that's Mr. Briggs's problem. It's not your problem, Mr. Barnes. And it's not Miss Elcock's.

"I spent the whole morning getting that Gallery in shape. The hooks are up. The labels up. The spotlights adjusted to the dimensions of each frame. So you see, Mr. Barnes, we're as ready as we can be .... No, they can't use any of our men. Because of the insurance. Our policy doesn't go into effect until Art Express's paintings are actually hanging on our walls.

"Now if anything comes up, you get in touch with me, you hear? Nobody else but me. I'm driving to the Hopkinsville Airport now. You can page me there, if you need me."

Two hours later, swaying on the arm of the Governor,

Eileen waited for her husband to open the door of their Mercedes. She was wearing her new dress, an extravagance from Bergdorf's custom cut to her plumpness from a gold-threaded Oriental fabric.

"I'll sit in the back," she said. "Beside the Governor."

"Suits me," Harry said. And stretching his neck to avoid the starch on his tuxedo shirt, he jerked open the back door.

"We'll let Harry be the chauffeur," Eileen said as she swung her hips into the car, then gently lifted in her legs, pointing her toes to show her ankles to advantage.

The Governor, a hefty, wheezing man of 60, fell in after her.

"Watch your hands," Harry shouted as he slammed the door behind them. Then he walked around to the driver's seat, tossing his keys in the air.

A moment later the diesel engine roared and the Mercedes leapt forward just as a loud speaker crackled and coughed up a voice: "Paging Mrs. Reeves. Mrs. Harry Reeves. A message for Mrs. Reeves at the Information Desk."

By the time the speaker had crackled back to silence, the Mercedes had diminished to a small metallic speck passing through the gate of the airport parking lot.

At five minutes after six the Mercedes slid to a stop in front of a windowless brick building surrounded by a lawn of freshly seeded topsoil roped off from a flagstone path and terrace.

A crowd had already gathered on the terrace: ladies in long dresses and men in dinner jackets, laughing, chatting, and sipping champagne from long-stemmed glasses while a canopy of cigarette smoke undulated lazily above their heads.

What a perfectly beautiful crowd, Eileen thought to herself as she walked toward the terrace on the arm of the Governor. Hard as I have worked for it, I never really thought I'd see it here in Surrey.

Suddenly, from the blurred scene on the terrace, a single figure leapt out like a typographical error. Oh my Lord, Jean Elcock! In a drab little print, with a V neckline. Nobody that flat-chested should ever wear that neckline.

"I've got to talk to you, Mrs. Reeves." Behind her contact lenses, which gave her a rather startled expression, Jean Elcock's ash-gray eyes were smouldering with anger. "Mr. Barnes won't let me into the Gallery. He says you gave him orders not to let me in."

"I'll explain it … later," Eileen whispered from the corner of her mouth as she flashed a wide smile at the President of Surrey Gravel and Granite. "Right now you've got to meet the Governor."

"Governor," Eileen said, pressing his arm gently. "There's someone here I want you to meet. My cochairman, Jean Elcock. Jean, may I present the Governor."

"Pleased to meet you, Miss Elcock," the Governor said as he squeezed the limp hand that was offered to him.

Before Jean Elcock could reply, Eileen interrupted: "The Mayor's signaling! It's time to start."

For five long minutes, in front of a slab of driftwood into which the words "Winslow Homer, Painter of the Sea" had been irregularly burnt, the Governor spoke about the

Cultural Explosion. It had started in the urban centers of the East, he said. Then it had crossed the Alleghenies. Like the pioneers, it had rushed across the Alleghenies into the great cities of Louisville and Lexington. And now it was appearing in smaller towns, like Surrey. But no city, large or small, can have a cultural explosion unless there is a special someone to ignite it. And we should all be thankful that Surrey had that someone. That necessary spark of creativity. Without further ado he would like to recognize that someone, that very charming someone, the creative spark of Surrey, Mrs. Harry Reeves.

Eileen stepped forward then, carrying a pair of scissors adorned with a large red satin bow. "Thank you," she said, nodding to the speaker with the poise of a woman who is used to compliments. "Thank you," she said, nodding to the crowd. "And especially I want to thank my cochairman, Professor Jean Elcock from Surrey Community College. She has been an enormous help to me in preparing this exhibition. Our premiere exhibition: "Winslow Homer, Painter of the Sea." Now that all the work is done, I must confess to you that if I had not had Miss Elcock's help I would have been at sea myself."

As soon as the ripple of laughter subsided, Eileen handed the shears to the Governor, who pried them open over a red ribbon that was stretched across the entrance to the Gallery. Then he snapped the shears together, and the ribbon fluttered, in two pieces, to the floor.

Instantly the crowd surged forward, led by Miss Elcock, through a threshold of bleached boards that were meant to suggest a humble fisherman's hut.

Eileen and the Governor stopped at the threshold to shake hands. Here comes Justice Stone, Eileen thought, clenching her teeth to contain a sudden rush of satisfaction. Two years ago he told me he wouldn't be caught dead inside an art museum.... And the Methodist minister's wife. I wonder if she drank champagne .... And old Mrs. Pritchett who never deigns to come to the Children's Infirmary Ball....

Suddenly, a shrill voice severed her contentment. A familiar voice. Oh my Lord, she thought. That's Jean Elcock's voice.

"They're not here!" Jean Elcock shrieked. "You've got to stop this right away. They're not here!"

Eileen took a deep breath and then exhaled her words, one by one. "*Who* is not here?" she said.

"The paintings, you idiot. The Winslow Homer paintings. The truck broke down in Putney. The paintings haven't come!"

Eileen felt something break loose, then fall inside her rib cage as if her heart had dropped through a trap door. Numbly she released whatever hand she had been shaking and pushed her way into the gallery, elbowing through the forest of tuxedos that was blocking her view.

At one point her shin struck a piece of barnacled driftwood. Then she almost fell over a lobster pot. But finally she managed to reach the fishnet room divider which she yanked aside to get a view of the Gallery wall. What she saw there was a starkly simple pattern — a pattern of sea-green labels alternating with empty rectangles of light.

Eileen turned around then and looked at the faces. She felt a little better when she looked at the faces, for they were flushed from the champagne and apparently contented. In fact, it crossed her mind that a photograph of the faces with the fishing nets behind them would do very well on a brochure of the Museum. Some were reading the information panels; others were studying the seashells; and still others were smiling from the simple pleasure of being part of such a crowd. Now and then there was a face that registered a question, a slight hint of anticipation not yet satisfied, but on the whole there was no sign of deep distress except that every 30 seconds the fog horn — which Eileen had traveled to Maine to record on the finest tape recorder that money could buy — let out a long and desperately lonely moan.

Hugh

I am standing on the terrace of the Alumnae House, listening to a classmate from Pem East whom I remember chiefly for her gentle wit and acne — which has cleared up completely after 25 years — and the egg stains on her pale blue woolen bathrobe.

Suddenly I notice a familiar face from the Class of '47. (They're the ones with owl-shaped name tags; ours are round with "25th" in large Gothic print.) It is a fairly long face, with a nose that is too large for the close-set eyes above it and skin that has been leathered by the sun. From the simple dress the woman's wearing — lime green linen — and gold bracelets on her wrists, I can tell she's rich and social — the Miss Porter's type that always slightly frightened me.

As she leans her shingled gray head back to laugh, she shows a set of teeth which bite into my memory so deeply that I wince with pain. The same kind of pain I felt this morning when I walked through Pembroke Arch and passed the bicycle rack I fell backward over once when Hugh Patterson — the only man I've ever loved in the reckless, headlong way that Cathy loved Heathcliff — was kissing me goodnight.

I fell, sad to say, not from the force of his passion, but from clumsiness. Absent-mindedness. Not noticing the thing was there.

A chaste peck on the cheek was all Hugh Patterson ever offered me in Pembroke Arch, though around us other couples writhed like tangled worms beside the bicycles or beneath the limestone owls that stared down from a shield with the motto: *Veritatem Dilexi*: "I chose truth."

A rather sad choice I have always thought. And I use the word "sad" the way my mother, a former member of the Sweet Briar May Court, uses it: "She's a nice girl, really. It's a shame that she's so sad." Because it was her firm belief, halfway passed along to me, that Bryn Mawr girls chose truth because they didn't have a better option.

"But I didn't take the job," my classmate's saying now. "Because I need some time, you see. I've just been through the grueling, if useless, ordeal of the Ph.D. Raised three children and lost one. I'm 46 years old and I have this premonition — if I can give myself a little time this summer, I just may be about to grow up!"

We all laugh at that remark. Me included, though I'm still staring at the teeth of that woman from the Class of '47, moving the unique shape of them across the jigsaw puzzle of my past. Suddenly, they fall right into place. She's Hugh Patterson's cousin. Or, more accurately, the rich girl from the Main Line (was it Bailey, Banks, or Biddle?) who married his cousin. Generally, Hugh's family was as hard up as mine was. But he did have this one cousin who was married to a rich girl with a farm out in Paoli. It had fieldstone fences, I remember, and a long, thin swimming pool, and best of all, a pond where Hugh would take me ice skating at night.

A wave of undiluted longing for Hugh Patterson washes over me. I see him kneeling in pine needles, lacing up my ice skates, his tight blond curls so close to my knee that I can easily reach out and run my fingers through them. But I know, of course, I mustn't. The basis of my strategy — my Five Year Plan to win him — is to hold back all this feeling, since he measures out his love for me in demitasse spoons.

So I have to be content to anticipate the moment, not very far away now, when he'll knot the laces, pull me to my feet and slip his arm around my waist where it will burn through my wool sweaters, as we wobble down the bank in silence. Then step onto the moonlit, pine-fringed pond of ice.

Helen is her name.

My eyes are still OK for reading at a distance, so I work them like two plumber's snakes around the bodies that block me from the woman's name tag. Before I have a chance to read it, a tanned arm reaches across it.

Twenty-two years I have waited to find out what has happened to Hugh Patterson. Here, at last, may be a woman who can tell me. My patience at this moment is inexhaustible. Eventually, that arm will move away.

In the meantime I will stand here, pretending that I'm listening to my classmate's chatter, for this time I am determined to make contact with Hugh.

At my tenth reunion I passed up a chance to see him. Back then one of my classmates — long since divorced and moved with her four children to California — lived down the street from him in a section of Philadelphia called Fairmount that was just then beginning to be restored. She told me they were having a neighborhood street fair the Sunday afternoon of our tenth reunion weekend and that Hugh was going to be the auctioneer. What I ought to do, she said, was stop off at the street fair on my way back to the airport. That way I was bound to see him.

I played with the idea all weekend long, imagining Hugh's face when I stood up at the auction, rehearsing what I'd say when we ducked into a restaurant afterwards to have a drink together. I'd heard rumors that he'd taken up with a Swarthmore girl five years older than he was; that at one point he was actually living with her, unusual in those days, for Hugh particularly, who cared so much about appearances and had been agonizingly celibate with me.

The arm has moved away now, but the woman in the green dress has turned her body slightly. I still can't see the name tag.

In my fantasies, over tenth reunion weekend, I discounted the rumors. Or rather, I decided that if that older woman did exist, she would be out of town. It was only fair that Hugh and I should have one final talk during which I could finally justify my actions to him.

Actions that most certainly did not deserve the box he'd sent by parcel post the week after my engagement was announced. When the mailman brought it to the door, I assumed it was a wedding present. I ran back to the dining room, got the carving knife and cut the package open right there in the hall. Out spilled the mementos from the five years Hugh and I had known each other. Theater programs from ballets and plays that we had seen together. The expensive leather belt — with his initials on the buckle — I'd given him one Christmas. Even the five-pound rock we brought home from a hike in the Poconos because we both admired its striated colors. He was going to use it as a doorstop in the house he had just bought in Fairmount to restore.

I was stunned by this evidence of bitterness from a man who almost never showed emotion. And embarrassed, deeply, for Hugh and for myself.

I put the things back in the box, before anybody in my family could see them, lugged it out to the garbage can, then went up to my room and wept. If Hugh had shown that much feeling two months earlier, none of this would be happening, I thought. I'd be engaged to him instead. Then suddenly my head popped up from the tear-soaked pillow. Hey, wait a minute. Where were all my letters?

The crafty bastard. He was still saving my letters — on the slim chance that I might fulfill my rapidly diminishing potential and become a famous poet after all. Then he could step forward and reveal to the world that he was the one I had lavished my first fine careless rapture on. Or maybe he was hoping he could sell the letters. God dammit, I thought, it's almost worth the effort of becoming famous to find out what Hugh will do with all my letters.

Even in this final gesture, Hugh could not bring himself to go all the way. And that fact took the sting out of the gesture. Made it easier for me to tell Sam about it when he took me out that night. Actually, I'd found that I could tell Sam anything, which was one reason that I felt relaxed, if not particularly happy, about the fact that I was going to marry him.

But I would not have told Sam if I had stopped off to see Hugh on the way back from my tenth reunion. And it would have been the first time I had deliberately held something back from him. In the end I didn't go; I took the limousine straight to the airport.

It was probably too soon for me to see Hugh anyway. I

was still getting postcards signed "As ever, Hugh" which drove Sam up the wall. He had always understood how strong my love for Hugh was, even if Hugh didn't. And I guess I was afraid of Sam's reaction. Maybe even more afraid of my own. For there was always that small chance that if I heard Hugh's voice again, it would catch me like a fish hook in the heart. And there I'd be — in the same old situation — using every ounce of wit and energy to keep the hook from tearing any further, following so fast, to keep the line of pain that tied me to him slack, that I appeared to be moving on my own.

If the hook sank deep enough, it might mean that I would have to leave Sam. And probably, my children, too. And I truly loved my children, though by that time I knew that I would never love Sam the way that I'd loved Hugh.

What I felt for Sam was much more basic. Sam could never be called handsome, except, perhaps, when his brown eyes are burning with a new idea, or amusement at the human situation. He has a dime-size bald spot on the back of his black head which has spread over the years to the size of a golf ball — an emblem of his own mortality I find particularly poignant since he can't see it himself. What I felt for Sam was too day-in-and-out — quotidian would be the word — to work up to the Olympian intensity of my love for Hugh.

If I had seen Hugh then, I might have had to leave, not only Sam, but my children, too. For how could Hugh put up with my runny-nosed, poorly disciplined, frequently nauseated children? I remembered all too well the night he explained to me why he'd decided to switch from general surgery to ophthalmology:

"Because I'm sick of all those people vomiting," he said. "And — if you want to know the truth — I'm also sick of blood."

I figured he was overworked, half kidding when he said that, since it was the middle of his intern year and he was averaging less than four hours of sleep a night. But he was serious. The very next week he took the necessary steps to change his field to ophthalmology.

The eye — he explained, another night when we were necking in his mother's car — the eye seemed to be detached from the rest of the body. Aesthetically interesting. Elegantly fashioned. More appealing, surely, as a lifetime's work, than bursting bowels or spurting arteries.

By the time that tenth reunion came around my youngest child was nine months old; my oldest, barely six. I was absolutely mired in blood and vomit. And I figured that if Hugh swept me off my feet and back into his life again, he might very well refuse to take my children. Even though my oldest daughter and my youngest son are blond.

I remember how he used to say, as if it were a joke, "I can't help it, Tompkins." He sometimes called me Tompkins, as my roommate, Harriet, and the hockey coach did; it made me feel that I was still a long-legged, sexless schoolgirl. "God knows I've tried, but I just can't help it, Tompkins. As a rule, I like blondes best." And there was absolutely no way — short of wigs or bleach — that I could ever be a blonde, though I did point out that I had been a blonde as a child and the chances were my children would be, too.

The only time Hugh came to visit me — in New York, two years before my parents moved back to Virginia —

I made him look through a book of photographs of my sister and myself as children. "See there, I'm the smallest one. The blonde one. Sitting on the swing." I even engineered an evening at my sister's apartment, ostensibly so that Hugh could meet her husband, a neurology resident at Bellevue, but actually to show him that my niece was blonde, although both of her parents had hair that was darker than mine.

It was pitiful. The way I dragged him down to Peter Cooper Village, changing from the E train to the BMT and then a crosstown bus, to impress on him the fact that I was probably carrying a recessive gene that could give him what he wanted. Beautiful blonde daughters.

By the time we got there, my niece was asleep. So I marched Hugh back into her bedroom and woke the poor child up, and she stood there at the crib rail in her feet pajamas, rubbing sleep from her blue eyes and shaking that bright golden head that was meant to serve as proof that I could be the mother of blonde daughters.

And do you know what Hugh said when he saw her? "I think she has inherited the tendency toward strabismus. That means slightly crossed eyes which can produce a condition called amblyopia — the loss of sight in one eye. You should tell your sister to have her eyes examined. Right away."

Two of my own children have inherited the tendency toward strabismus. The youngest one, Sammy, had to have an eye muscle clipped when he was barely four years old. I remember how he stood there by that hospital bed that was taller than he was, his short, plump toes sticking out from his seersucker pajamas, while Sam and I listened to the casters of the stretcher coming down the hall to take him off to Surgery.

His cornflower blue eyes looked up through the lenses of his horn-rimmed glasses, as he said: "Dr. Cary's gonna move my eye. Right, Daddy? Right, Momma?" Then softly, to himself, "He's gonna move my eye. But just a little bit."

When the orderly came in, he took Sammy's glasses off and set them on the night table against the water pitcher. Then he hooked his thumbs under Sammy's armpits, swung him up onto the stretcher, and rolled him from the room.

For the next two hours, while Sam tried to read a book and I, a newspaper, those tiny horn-rimmed glasses, propped against that water pitcher, stared at me, reproaching me for my genetic flaw, for my stupidity in not taking Sammy to the eye doctor sooner, for all the unnamed failures that mothers carry around with them like birdshot in the heart.

My children have that awful power that Hugh once had of absorbing me completely. And in the process wrecking all my plans.

Back when I was in high school — and my freshman year in college — those plans were all I had. And as long as that was so, anything I put my mind to I could do. But then one February afternoon my sophomore year, I looked up from a snowball fight outside of Pembroke West and saw Hugh Patterson's profile. And a voice inside me said with quiet certainty, "That's the man I want to marry."

It was a sign of things to come that Hugh did not notice me as he stopped one of my friends to ask where Bitsy Smith, a girl he'd met in Europe, lived.

His eyes, I noticed, were a pale, transparent blue, and

as he talked, he held them open wide, as if surprised and slightly shocked by what they saw; yet through them came no clues to what he might be feeling. His nose was short and straight with a sudden childish up-tilt at the end, which had the same effect on me as the snubbed nose of a puppy. It made me want to hug him. But what really tore my heart that afternoon and claimed the next five years of my life was the sight of his sharp-peaked, perfectly formed lips which, when he wasn't speaking, he kept pressed together, as if holding back some sorrow that he could not talk about.

I loved Hugh instantly, and decided I was probably the only person in the world who could draw that sorrow from him. Suddenly I was possessed with a joyful sense of mission. My only problem now was how could I get close enough to him to do the job?

Luckily, Bitsy Smith — the girl he'd come to see — was already engaged to a law student at Penn. So later that same afternoon I dropped by Bitsy's suite and joined the crowd that was having tea and cocoa by her fire. I'd hoped to find Hugh there, but by that time he had left. So I took Bitsy aside and asked if she would fix me up with him sometime.

I "set my cap" for Hugh, as my grandmother would put it. She was much more optimistic about my chances for success with men than Mother, who thought I was too smart for my own good. Nana's theory was that everything depends on strategy. "Any woman but a hunchback can get the man she wants," she said, and I believed her, deeply grateful that although I'd never be a beauty, with my long face and flat chest, I did not have a hunchback. Moreover, I had damn good-looking legs.

There would be times, of course, during the next five years

when I questioned Nana's wisdom. The more schemes I devised to show Hugh why he ought to marry me, the more reasons he found why he should not. It was only after I gave up that he came around to almost asking me.

And by that time I'd met Sam. He had slipped into my life the summer I was living with my parents between two teaching jobs. I started going out with him on weekdays — when I couldn't see Hugh — because I liked to be around him. He was so affirmative and interested in everything around him — politics and history and people. I couldn't help but notice the contrast between Hugh's mincing progress and Sam's reckless careening toward commitment, his eagerness to offer me everything he was and would be, accepting in return anything I had to offer, including the possibility that I might never love him.

It nearly broke my heart to watch Hugh work around to the conclusion that I was probably the best that he could get. I could almost hear him thinking: "Her hair may be brown and her genes ambylopic, but she is well educated, sensitive to the arts, and surprisingly effective socially" as he proceeded, step by cautious step, to the point that he could tell me he was "looking for engagement rings" though he still could not come right out and say who the ring was for. Me, obviously. Wasn't I the only girl he was dating?

When he started all that talk about engagement rings, I could easily have asked him: "Who is the ring for?" But by that time, I was trapped in my own strategy of indirection. Fearful, too, that if I chose the wrong words — honest, blunt, direct words — he would vanish.

As he had vanished once — for my entire senior year — after he had forced me to stand up to him in public.

It happened at a dinner dance that Hugh's class, the junior class, at the medical school was giving for the seniors. One of Hugh's classmates took out a cigar and asked me if I'd like to try it. I debated for a second, then decided to say no. But before I could speak, Hugh said, "Don't smoke that cigar."

Then he announced in the silence that had settled on the table, "I swear to you, Tompkins, if you so much as take a puff from that cigar, I'll never take you out again in my whole life."

The words knocked the breath out of my lungs; I felt as if I'd come down from a high jump and landed on my arm. All I could do at first was gasp to get the air back. By the time I was breathing normally again, I knew I had to smoke the damn cigar. Or give in to Hugh completely. Either way I'd lose him. So I might as well lose him with my pride intact.

I did not answer him. Instead I reached across the heavy-duty tablecloth — by now ringed with stains from our drinks and smudged with ashes from our cigarettes — and plucked the cigar from Hugh's classmate's fingers, brought it over to my mouth and took two puffs from it. Then I passed it back to him — all in total silence, since everybody there, with the possible exception of Hugh, himself, knew how much those two puffs cost.

For the rest of the evening Hugh was exceedingly polite. And when the dance was over, he drove me home in silence, walked me to the door of Pembroke East, and bowed out of my life for a whole year.

The following September I looked for him at the Freshman mixer, which the medical school students usually came to. Finally, one of his friends asked me to dance and told me Hugh had gone to Edinburgh for the year on a research fellowship. It was March before Hugh wrote me. And July before I saw him, at which time neither one of us mentioned that cigar.

It had earned me, by the way, a modest fame at the medical school, which provided me with dates to pass the time my senior year. But I had no interest in them. If I couldn't have Hugh, I really did not want another man. Instead, I threw myself into my work, and to the horror of my mother — my grandmother had died before her strategy had worked — graduated first among the English majors, had a poem accepted by a major literary magazine, and won a fellowship to study medieval drama at Cambridge.

Ironically, it was these accomplishments, added to the fact that I had survived without him, that drew Hugh back to me, I think. I delayed sailing to Europe, so that I could see him for another month. And did not apply for a renewal of my Fulbright, but came right back across the ocean to a mediocre job, teaching English and Latin at a private girls' school, just to be in Philadelphia where he was.

And it almost worked. In fact there was a time — twelve blissful hours — when I thought that I had finally won him.

It happened on a Saturday in mid-December, the day before I was to take the train back to Virginia to spend the week of Christmas with my parents, Hugh had the whole day off, so he borrowed his mother's car and drove out to the house in Ardmore I was sharing with two girls who taught at Shipley with me.

He arrived in faded jeans and a ski parka, with a cleaner's bag over his arm. "Guess what?" he said. "We've got free tickets to a dinner dance tonight at the Radnor Hunt Club. I've got my tuxedo. Have you got an evening dress?"

"I've got a bridesmaid's dress," I said. The fact was I had several; that was the year so many of my friends were getting married. I was planning to cook dinner for Hugh there, at the house, since both of my housemates were going to be out. Yet I could tell he really wanted to go to that dance, even though there would be no one there we knew. Still, it was a free dinner. Better yet, a chance to dance with Hugh all evening long.

Hugh was a magnificent dancer. His tall, bony body always seemed to know what it was doing on the dance floor; and it managed to communicate that knowledge to mine. Whenever we assumed the ballroom dance position, with one arm at the other's waist, the other stretched out almost straight, I marveled at the way our long bodies fit together. And as we started dancing we would press our bodies closer till the rhythm of the music merged them into one.

My most recent bridesmaid's dress, smartly tailored in peach-colored organdy, was surprisingly becoming. Hugh had never seen it. The more I thought about that dress and the prospect of going to a dance with him that night, the more I warmed to the idea.

We spent the afternoon working on separate projects in my third-floor attic bedroom. For my birthday Hugh had given me a pine tavern table to use as a writing table. One Sunday afternoon we had driven all the way to the town of York, to a warehouse for antiques, to pick it out. And he had promised to refinish it for me on his afternoons off. We kept the tavern table and his electric sander in my bedroom, so that he could close the door whenever he was sanding and keep the dust from spreading through the house.

Every surface of my bedroom — the floor, the window sills, the jar-tops on my bureau — were coated with a saffron-colored dust, and my clothes and blankets smelled of ground-up varnish. But I loved to have Hugh there, doing his work at one end of the room, while I sat in the middle, at a rickety card table, doing mine.

On this particular day I was planning the assignments for my tenth grade English class. And Hugh was lying on the floor, with his long legs folded up, like a grasshopper's, working on the underside of the tavern table. It was almost as communal as being married.

Except there was one difference. One enormous difference. In our tortured attitude toward my bed. The presence of that bed — tucked under the eaves at the far end of the room — made us both exquisitely uneasy. And we took great care to avoid even a glance in that direction.

In this respect, I felt a little less than honest. I had had far more experience with beds and sex than Hugh suspected, even though I was, like most of my friends, still technically a virgin. But Hugh blithely assumed that since I was four years younger, I must be four years more innocent than he.

It did not occur to me — concentrating all my thoughts on my strategy to win him — that my experience might be something Hugh could use, something Hugh might need. I was, in fact, reluctant to reveal it. In retrospect, it's hard to reconstruct my elaborately fabricated attitude toward sex then. But I do remember this much. When I read the end of the best seller, *Marjorie Morningstar*, where the fiancé threatens to call the wedding off because he's learned that the heroine is not a virgin, I did not get the point — that this attitude reflected on his character, not hers. I thought he had a perfect right to drop her.

Besides, that afternoon I experienced a pleasure that can come when one has to refrain from sex which surpassed any pleasure I had yet received from yielding to it. We were on our honor not to misbehave in my bedroom. For me, it was as if I were back in my dormitory room with an unfinished exam book on my desk and a textbook on the shelf with the answers in it. The very proximity of the opportunity made it impossible to consider yielding to it. This was a moral test; if I cracked open the textbook, or fell onto the bed with Hugh, I would forfeit my ability to like myself.

Or so I thought, when Hugh dragged his bentwood chair up to the card table by mine — pulling the round wooden seat through the trim crotch of his jeans and sitting so close to me that his denim-covered thigh rested against mine. A liquid warmth slid through my body, as if I had just swallowed a mouthful of strong brandy. And I felt suddenly limp with longing for him.

"What are you giving them to read?" he asked as he bent over my papers. Hugh liked to read even more, perhaps, than I did, since he read purely for pleasure, while I read for my living now. As he hunched over the table, hugging his bony elbows, his posture struck me as inordinately boyish.

"Aren't you skimping on my hero, Henry James?" he asked. "Just those two short stories? Why don't you give them *Portrait of a Lady*?"

"It's too long," I said. "If you want to know the truth, I've never finished it, myself."

"Oh, you've got to, Tompkins! It's a *wonderful* book.

Practically equal to a trip to England, First Class, with the perfect guide. And visually, it beats the Barnes Collection. It's probably my favorite book." He paused. "How can I marry you if you won't even read my favorite book?"

I never knew how to respond when Hugh began to joke about the subject I considered so important. I didn't answer him.

"At least I'm glad to see you're giving a whole week to Emily Dickinson."

"But I can't decide which poems. Have you got any suggestions?"

"Will you really let me choose them?" he asked, delighted as a child would be. It was this hint of innocence, a core of innocence, that made me love Hugh most, I think.

He picked up my small Modern Library edition of the poems, propped it open on his knees at the Index of First Lines and began to check the poems he liked.

Later, after I had finished dressing for the dance and was waiting through that block of time before a date when a girl is too carefully coiffed and powdered to do anything useful, I had a chance to look over his choices. I was shocked to discover that every single one of them dealt with death.

As we were driving to the dance, I asked him: "Do you realize that those poems you checked are all about death?"

"That's not so!" he said. "I know I checked 'The Soul Selects Her Own Society.' And that's a love poem, don't you think?"

" 'I've known her from an ample nation/Choose one;/ Then close the valves of her attention/Like stone?' Don't those lines suggest a cemetery vault to you?"

"A bank vault," he said.

"A *stone* bank vault? And what about 'I Heard a Fly Buzz When I Died'...'Because I Could Not Stop for Death'...?"

"OK, OK. You win," he said. "Obviously I have a ghoulish streak in me. Now that you have forced me to the truth." He turned from the steering wheel to leer at me in the moonlight that was sifting through the windshield, "I'll tell you my dark secret. The fact is I'm a *vampire*, cleverly disguised as a would-be doctor."

On the way back from the dance, though, he brought the subject up again. At that point in the evening, those poems were the last thing on my mind. I was still basking in my unexpected success at the Radnor Hunt Club dance, where several Main Line bachelors who used to take out friends of mine from Pembroke East kept cutting in on me to find out what had happened to the girls they used to date. Each time one of them did, and Hugh came back to me, our long bodies would lock, and the pleasure we derived as they dipped across the dance floor seemed to have been intensified, rather than diminished, by the brief, involuntary separation. For once we did not even feel the need to talk.

I was still suspended in that totally relaxed and satisfied silence which we'd managed to carry from the dance into the car, when Hugh said, "I've been thinking about what you said on the way over. I guess the reason that I checked those particular poems is that death — my father's death — is the most important thing that's happened to me yet."

Then in a steady voice, he started telling me what it had been like the day his father shot himself while he was cleaning some old guns. It happened two days after Hugh's seventh birthday.

"He had given me a litter of puppies for my birthday.

Beagles. And was going to help me raise them and train for the hunt. I was down at the barn, playing with the puppies, when I heard the gun go off."

There was silence for a second, but this time it was a silence that I felt unqualified to deal with. I had never experienced a sorrow even roughly comparable to this one.

When he spoke again, his voice was flatter and more guarded: "And to this day the smell of puppies — that sweet oniony smell of a puppy's breath — brings back all the bloody horror of that afternoon. It's positively Proustian, don't you agree?"

For once, I refused to follow his quickstep into intellectuality, as I would have followed the pressure of his hand on the small of my back, or his leg against my leg on the dance floor. I did not want this moment to degenerate so quickly into literary talk.

"I don't know," I said, "I've never had anything that awful happen to me. Did you train those puppies?"

"No," he said, "We sold them three months later when we sold the farm."

"But you still like dogs," I said. "It didn't turn you against dogs. You practically raised that last litter of beagles at your cousin's."

"That's true," he said. "And after I get married, I think I'd like to have a farm, myself."

"It was an accident, right?"

"Oh my God, yes," he said. "I can't believe he would have willed us into everything that happened after that."

We pulled up to a stoplight. "And now, Herr Doctor Tompkins, we have reached Lancaster Pike. Would you like to get a hamburger before I take you home?"

With that, we dropped the subject. But later when we pulled into the driveway behind my housemate's car, I abandoned my strategy for once and acted on an impulse. I slide over in the seat, slipped my arms around his waist, under his tuxedo coat, and hugged him.

He responded with a long, hard kiss. And when we broke from it, to breathe, I thought I heard him whisper, "I love you." But a truck was groaning up the hill below, and I wasn't sure.

"What did you say?" I asked.

He did not repeat it. Instead, he kissed me lightly on the tip of my nose, then harder on my ear, then on my lips again, until I began to feel the same warmth sliding through my body I had felt that afternoon. Only this time we weren't in my bedroom, bound by honor. We were in a parked car.

All the calculations that my roommate, Harriet, and I had worked out, sitting on the window sill of our living room at college, our feet firmly planted on the balcony outside, our cigarette ends glowing several inches from our fingers — all those rules about how far a girl could go and still not run the risk of being thought a slut, seemed suddenly self-serving. Artificial. Trivial. As Hugh's passion rose to meet mine and we fell back on the seat, I would have given anything to him.

If he had wanted it.

But in the middle of our lovemaking, he drew back and sat up straight behind the steering wheel, his white tuxedo shirt gleaming in the moonlight.

"It's all right, Hugh," I said.

"But it may not be all right tomorrow morning," he said

evenly, "If we've waited this long, we can wait a little longer."

Then he took me in his arms again, cupped one hand under my breast, and drew my hand into his lap. And held it there, hard, as he kissed me one last time.

"Now let's get out of here," he said, as he opened the car door.

Delirious with joy, I stumbled up the driveway, hand in hand with Hugh, and burst into the kitchen where my housemates and their dates were gathered round the TV set, hissing at some film clips of Senator McCarthy. At that moment I believed that Hugh and I were engaged.

But when I woke up the next morning, I was not so sure. Had I imagined that he said "I love you"?

Before I took the train home for Christmas vacation, I stopped off at the hospital and had lunch with Hugh in the cafeteria, hoping he would do or say something to confirm my sense of a commitment.

But he behaved as if the night before had never happened. He had been working nonstop since six o'clock that morning and was preoccupied with the problems he was having with a patient.

For Christmas, though, he sent me an extravagant present. A gold pin from Tiffany's, shaped like a tiny beagle. And he asked me to go skiing with him over New Year's weekend. But it turned out there was no snow. So we canceled the ski trip, and he worked New Year's weekend, covering for a friend whose wife had gone into labor prematurely.

The next thing I knew, the vacation was over, and I was working harder than I'd ever worked before. In addition to my full-time job at Shipley, I had signed up for two courses in graduate school. Three months of high-school teaching had made me realize that I would rather teach in college, and for that I was going to need some more degrees.

Hugh, poor thing, was even more overworked than I was. Since he was on call almost all the time, he would often get less than two hours of uninterrupted sleep at night. And when we managed to meet briefly at the hospital, the movies, or even at my house (where I sometimes had to leave him working on that tavern table while I rushed off to an evening seminar), we sat and stared at one another across a pool of mutual exhaustion.

I began to wonder if that night of the dance had ever happened.

"You were always so *sure*," he said that final weekend in New York, at Harriet's wedding. At that point Harriet and Hugh were the only people who knew that I'd decided to accept Sam's proposal. And Harriet threw her bouquet at me with so much force that I had to catch it, though I would have given anything not to have seen the expression on Hugh's face as the bouquet fell into my hands.

"You were always so *sure*," he said again, when we were back in Harriet's apartment, standing in her tiny kitchen because another bridesmaid and her fiancé — whom she would marry in a year and divorce in seven — were filling up the living room with a ferocious fight.

Beside two small gas burners and a chipped porcelain sink, we acted out our final scene, my face buried in Hugh's bony shoulder, my tears soaking through his shirt while he held me, lightly, and watched the large electric clock on the wall.

The fact that I had been so sure was apparently the thing that had held him back. And now that I'd decided to marry someone else, he could suddenly afford to show his feeling for me. And I, in turn, had nothing to lose by showing mine.

"You can't imagine what it's like," he said, "to have to argue for your life. Suppose I choose the wrong words? Then I lose it. Everything I've planned. It all means nothing now. You must know that, Tompkins. Surely you have noticed that when we're in a room with other people, you're the only one I see. The only one I want to talk to."

But I could not turn back now. If I did, Hugh might retreat again. And even if he didn't, if he went ahead and married me, I knew now how much another man could love me, what it was like to be able to help myself, greedily, to all the love I wanted, anytime I needed it. And knowing that, I did not think that I could live now on the meager rations Hugh would offer me.

At the time, though, I was choking on the sudden flood of feeling for Hugh, and now *from* Hugh, and could not explain a thing to him. So he thought I might recover from my impulse to marry Sam. Why else did he call on a Sunday morning, two weeks later, and announce that he was driving to Virginia to have a talk with me?

"Oh, Hugh. No," I said. "This is the day that I'm announcing my engagement."

"In that case," he said evenly. "There's no point in my coming. Is there?"

And those were the last words I heard him speak.

* * * *

Across the terrace, now, I see the woman turning her green linen torso, so that, finally, her owl-shaped name tag flashes into view: HELEN BAILEY PATTERSON, 1947.

Before I have a chance to think, I am striding straight across the terrace. Standing by the woman. Stretching out my arm to shake her hand.

I am appalled at my own gall. I never knew this woman, really. When Hugh took me to her farm, we would chat politely, for not one minute longer than was necessary, because we understood, even if the men did not, that we inhabited entirely different worlds. So there is no reason now — except the one huge reason, Hugh — for me to resurrect this accidental, obsolete acquaintance.

Yet I will not die without talking to Hugh, once.

So I say, "Hello, Helen. How *are* you?" in a swooping social voice I have never heard before. "I'm Margaret Tompkins Baker." Her flecked green eyes are glazed with lack of recognition. So I press on stupidly: "*Margie* Tompkins. Class of '57. I knew you way back in the fifties when your cousin Hugh and I used to come out to your farm."

"Oh, yes. Yes, indeed!" she says, and I detect a flicker behind the dull green gaze. "I know exactly who you are. Where are you living now?"

"In Virginia," I say. Then I notice a plump woman with an owl-shaped name tag bearing down on us with two full tea cups rattling and sloshing in their saucers. I get right to the point. "How is Hugh? Do you ever see him?"

"All the time," she says, "when he comes out to the farm. And he's fine. In fact, I'd say Hugh's thriving. He's assistant head of ophthalmology at Jefferson Hospital now. Did you know that? And into art projects, of course, all over Philadelphia. Restoration, too, in the Fairmount section, mainly. He's restored five houses over there. By now, it may be six."

"Is he married?"

"Hugh? Married?"

She pauses long enough to break the rhythm of her talk, to open a small hole where a person more adept than I am at Main Line understatement might be able to deposit a meaning. But what would that meaning be?

"I don't think Hugh is *interested* in getting married. He's much too involved in other things. You really ought to call him while you're here."

"Do you have his phone number? I think it's unlisted." Think. Hell, I *know* it is unlisted. At my 20th reunion I finally worked up the nerve to call him, slipped away from a class meeting and closed myself into a booth. But when I opened up the phone book to the page with Pattersons, Hugh's name was not there.

"Yes, I have it. Somewhere." Helen's freckled hand dives into her box-shaped pocketbook and retrieves a small red leather book. She thumbs through pale blue tissue-paper pages.

"Do you want the one at work? Or home?"

"The one at home," And then I realize that I have no paper in my pocketbook. A pencil, yes, but not a piece of paper. I will have to use a check, or better yet, the cover of my class reunion booklet.

As Helen starts to read the numbers, I pencil them lightly on the cover of my class reunion booklet. Very, very lightly. The first sign of my possibly adulterous intentions. I need to be able to erase the numbers, later.

"Here, Bailey. *Take* this," A tea cup suddenly appears between us.

But I have what I want now. "Thank you very much," I say and whirl away before Helen Bailey Patterson is obliged to introduce me to her friend.

The next thing I know I'm marching with an electric sense of purpose off the terrace, out of Wyndham, back through Pembroke Arch, and straight across the campus toward the single room in Denbigh they've assigned me for the weekend. Miracle of miracles, it has a telephone.

I am exhilarated now, because I have a secret. After 22 years of shared thoughts and sheets — even toothbrushes, if pressed — I've discovered how liberating one secret can be. This must be the reason that married people find affairs so tempting. What we need is not the sex so much as the affirmation that each of us is still a separate being.

I remember when our youngest son, Sammy, started nursery school, I found an unfamiliar-looking Matchbox truck in an ashtray and asked Will, the oldest, who was then about five, "Whose truck is this?"

"Sammy's. He brought it home from school."

"But where did Sammy get it?"

"I don't know," Will said solemnly. "I don't know Sammy's life."

His statement pierced my mind. Until that moment, I had known the origin of practically every toy Sammy touched and every word he uttered. Now, all of a sudden, he had a life outside our life, a constant source of secrets.

Now suddenly, at 46, I have a secret, too. I decide that I am game for whatever it may bring me. One secret breeds another, the way a little lie does, and may lead into a tangled situation. But at least it will be a different situation.

There was a time, five or six summers ago, when Sam considered having an affair with a young economist he was working with in New York City. She was single, bored, and liberated, and made him an offer with no strings attached. But he got drunk first and asked me would I mind.

Open Marriage was on the best-seller list then. Everyone was reading it, trading it between the beach chairs, and I had expressed fairly liberal opinions on the subject. But the night that Sam got drunk and asked me did I mean it, I found out I most certainly did *not*.

I tried to analyze my unbecomingly conservative reaction. What I minded most was the thought of an ongoing deception. Being made a fool of. Having Sam call me up from dinner with his mistress in a fancy New York restaurant, while I was stuck at home, eating fish sticks with the children. And having him pretend that he was sorry that his business was taking him out of town so much. He's a good sport, Sam. If he was considering having an affair himself, he figured it was only fair to talk to me about it, so that I could have one, too. Would I do the same for him? I hope so.

When I get to Denbigh, I walk straight up the steps into my room, deliberately avoiding contact with my classmates who are draped over the chairs and sofas in the Showcase, smoking, gossiping, and reminiscing.

But I do not try to make the call until I've had a bath and have almost finished dressing. My ride to our class dinner is leaving at six-thirty. Sam's quartz travel clock, on the scratched, fake-maple desktop, says almost six o'clock.

I will call Hugh now, I think. And I plop down on the metal cot to use the telephone.

A private telephone. Imagine. In my day, all we had to link us to the world of men was one pay phone and Venus, the legendary bell maid of Pembroke Hall.

Venus had had sleeping sickness once, and for that reason, she moved very slowly. When the switchboard downstairs started buzzing, she would squeeze herself into the tiny, glassed-in station, settle on the swivel chair and adjust the headphone. Carefully. So that the small black cup of it would hang just below her lower lip, ready to catch whatever slurred words should fall, one by one, like drops of water from an almost cut-off faucet.

Only then would she reach for a brass-tipped cord, pull it up and plug it into the small hole that was flashing with an incoming call. The buzzing suddenly would stop. There would be silence for a second. Then three syllables would drop into the plastic cup: "Pem-broke Hawl."

The caller would give the name of the student in either Pembroke East or West that he (or in some sad cases, she) wanted to talk to. And four more syllables would fall from Venus: "Just a min-ute." Which meant, of course, several minutes while she dragged another plug up from the board, where they sprouted in neat rows, like brass asparagus. Then she forced that plug into the hole that connected to the wall phone on the student's corridor. After that, she'd flip a worn black plastic switch, lean back in the chair and throw her arm out to a wallboard dotted with yellowing ivory buttons that had room numbers below them. Finally, her wrinkled forefinger would find the button that she needed and press down on it hard.

If the student happened to be sitting at her desk when the buzzer on her wall erupted, she would start up from her chair and race out to the wall phone on her floor, knowing just how long her caller had been waiting, fearing always that he would have given up by that time. Some boys did give up and made their dates by Western Union or drove out from Penn or down from Princeton on the chance the girls they wanted to take out would still be free on Saturday. And largely, thanks to Venus and the college's even-then-archaic communications system, it was a fairly good chance.

Our old phone system was tedious and maddening, but oh my God, it was exciting. When my wall buzzer came to life, my legs would react long before my mind did, carrying me halfway down the corridor before I started wondering: Who can that be calling? Oh dear God, please let it be Hugh. And if it was Hugh's voice, that thin, reeded, carefully articulated voice vibrating in my ear, I would collapse with pleasure, sliding down the rough, nubbed plaster wall to sit spreadeagled on the floor, surrendering to the ecstasy of talking to him, not caring that somebody down the hall was probably listening to our conversation, responding to the challenge of imagining the unheard half of it.

This private telephone, on the table here beside me, makes it seem too easy. Obscenely easy. To communicate with Hugh, all I have to do is pick up this receiver. Nobody will be listening, because I've taken the precaution of closing the door. I pick up the receiver, and dial the numbers lightly penciled on the cover of my class reunion booklet, as if they were no different from any other numbers.

I hear a click. Will Hugh be home at six o'clock? On a

Friday night? Then a distant ringing.

Suddenly he's with me. I know it is his voice that says "Hello?"

"Hugh! This is Margie. Margie Tompkins Baker ..." I meant to speak more slowly, but the words are sputtering. "I'm up here for my 25th reunion. So I thought I'd call you up and. ..."

He does not let me stumble any further.

"Good heavens. It is you. My God. I can't *believe* it. I was just thinking about you. You'll never guess where I was two weeks ago. In Virginia. In Williamsburg, no less. Giving a speech to the Southern Ophthalmologist's Association. In Williamsburg! Can you believe it? The very place I'd planned to give you an engagement ring. We were going to go to Williamsburg the weekend after Harriet's wedding. Do you remember that?"

"Yes, I remember."

"And I kept thinking about you the whole time I was there. So much so, I almost called you up."

His words are so unguarded, plunging all the way back into our old relationship. So why do I feel parried? By the timbre of his voice? The faint hint of laughter vibrating behind it. I never could tell for certain, and I cannot tell now, whether Hugh's laughter is ironic.

And why does he assume the role of the one who was rejected? Actually it's my role, and he's stealing it from me.

Is this what I have called him up to tell him? Clearly, he doesn't want to hear it. Any more than he wants to deal with me, the real, breathing me; I might destroy his artfully restored recollections. Hugh always did have a knack for making real things artificial. Once when I was taking a psychology course I gave him a Rorschach test for practice; and he kept saying, "That's a *picture* of a cat. That's a *picture* of a horse." Most people looking at the inkblots will say simply, "That's a cat," or "That's a horse." But Hugh insisted even then on distancing.

What I have failed to recognize all these years is that Hugh prefers to keep it all out there — just beyond his reach — clean and cerebral while the rest of us slosh through the juices — semen, blood, and vomit. He has a mind too fine to mire in an ordinary physical commitment.

This knowledge settles like a ball of dough at the bottom of my stomach, as I chatter on. Answering his questions. Downplaying my children. My four wonderful children. For where are his? Those beautiful blonde daughters I was secretly afraid I could not give him? They may never now exist outside of Hugh's mind, where they roam forever fair and free of acne.

And I am sad that this is so.

He is chatting, happily, telling me about the party he is going to give tomorrow, a buffet dinner for 40 people.

"Are you doing it all by yourself?" I ask.

"Yes," he says, "with the help of a few friends. Tonight they're coming over to tear up the lettuce for the salad. Tomorrow they will worry with the meat." It has something to do with a fine-arts center opening, at which Hugh says, "We're having carriage rides, no less."

I have absolutely no desire to come to his dinner party. Or to ride beside him in a carriage. And he has clearly no desire to ask me to.

The fact is, Hugh and I will never meet again, though we are pretending that we will. To be polite, he asks me for my married name. Can he really have forgotten it? Obligingly I give him Sam's full name, and our telephone number, and urge him to get in touch with us the next time he is down our way.

I say good-bye to Hugh then. And wait until I hear the click of his receiver, imagining the scene at his latest Fairmount town house.

His tightly curled blond hair is mixed with gray. Otherwise he is as handsome as he was the night we parted in that tiny New York kitchen. He's been sitting in a wing chair talking on the telephone, but he gets up from it now, and walks over to a bookcase and pulls out a volume of stories by his favorite author, Henry James.

He settles back into the wing chair, opening the book at "The Lesson of the Master," or, better yet, "The Jolly Corner." Then, as he starts to read, his long fingers reach for the stem of the wineglass beside him, not because he wants to drink from it, but just to reassure himself that it is there.

War Hero

As I stood there with my mother at Byrd Field, watching his khaki-colored plane grow larger in the sky, all I could think about was how my classmates envied me. "Lucky duck," Weezie said, "It's a real-life episode from 'Mary Noble, Backstage Wife'."

That was the radio program the fourth grade was deeply involved with. At this point in the story, Mary Noble was about to go on stage without knowing that her husband, who she thinks is still a Prisoner of War in Germany, is actually sitting in the audience. What's Mary going to do when she looks over the footlights and sees the man she loves? Will she scream? Will she faint? Or will she jump down from the stage and give him one of those long kisses Judy Garland gave to Robert Walker while they waited for his troop train to pull out of the station?

We were just about to die from the suspense. And for the past two weeks we'd been taking turns playing sick — tricking our mothers with thermometers we'd held under hot water — so that one of us could always stay home and listen to the program. And bring the others up to date on the playground the next day.

Now, all of a sudden, I had my own war hero. His name was Henry Carter, Major General Henry Carter Marshall. He was my mother's cousin and a member of MacArthur's staff. This hot summer afternoon in 1943 he was coming all the way from Australia to Richmond on a Secret Mission, "which just might be the thing that saves the War in the Pacific," the family's other general, mother's uncle and a hero from World War I, General Henry Pembroke Marshall, had said on the telephone the night before.

The khaki-colored plane had landed on the runway and was rolling toward us now, its propellers stirring up a wind that blew our skirts against our shins. Inside it was the war hero who would later meet a wife he hadn't seen for two long years — not since she'd been evacuated from the Philippines with the other army wives, right after Pearl Harbor. The husbands had stayed on to fight with General MacArthur as he was driven back from Manila through Bataan to re-establish his headquarters in Australia.

The wife's name was Eleanor. Though I'd never laid eyes on her, I imagined she was beautiful. And thin.

Henry Carter, it turned out, was just a little bit fat. I noticed it the minute he stepped into the doorway of that Army airplane. But when he leaned down to kiss me, he had the nicest eyes I'd ever seen. Very, very pale blue eyes. So kind and watery and sad I could not imagine them matching up the cross hairs on a gunsight.

They almost made up for the fact that half an hour later, he got stuck twice as Mother and I tried to boost him through the kitchen window because she'd locked the latch key in the house.

When he got through, finally, and opened up the door for us, Mother reached under the sink and brought out the pint of bourbon she'd traded in her coupons for that morning. Then she dropped some ice cubes in three glasses, poured Truade in one for me, and bourbon in the others.

"Now let's take our drinks into the living room," she said, "where we can sit beside the fan and decide just what we're going to do."

About Eleanor, that is.

Eleanor was Missing.

She hadn't gotten off the train we met at Main Street Station before we drove out to the airport to meet Henry Carter. So, Mother called her Uncle Henry in Washington, D.C. the oldest and the smartest member of her branch of the family. Everybody called him when they had a crisis. And, generally, he fixed it.

This time though she had to call him at his office, not his house, and had a hard time getting through. I know because I listened on the upstairs extension.

"Pentagon," said a mannish, woman's voice.

"I'd like to speak to General Marshall," Mother said.

"Which General Marshall?"

"General *Henry* Marshall."

"Which General Henry Marshall?"

"General Henry *Pembroke* Marshall."

"And who are you?"

"I'm his niece. And I really have to speak to him. It's an emergency," she said, steadying her voice. "Involving the Army. A special Mission of the Army."

After that, they let her through to tell her Uncle Henry that Eleanor had not been on the train from Petersburg though Uncle Henry's daughter had telephoned that morning to say she had put Eleanor on the Pocahontas. That's the morning train from Norfolk west to Roanoke which connects in Petersburg with a Northbound train to Richmond.

Silence crackled on the phone.

Then Mother's Uncle Henry said, "I don't suspect foul play."

Pictures flickered through my mind — slant-eyed saboteurs crawling on their bellies through grass blades big as bayonets in Suffolk, then leaping up onto the cars of the passing Pocahontas to kidnap the American general's wife and divert him from his Mission.

"No," said Mother's Uncle Henry. "There's no reason to suspect foul play, at this point. What's more likely is that Eleanor is drunk. And she's slept through her connection. Or gotten off in Petersburg and on to a train going South instead of North."

"Just keep calm," he said to Mother. "You go on to the airport and meet Henry Carter. Meanwhile I will get the Secret Service to track down Eleanor, and I'll call you when we've found her.

As I sat sipping Truade, letting the breeze from the fan cool the perspiration on my arm, I thought, "Please God, let Eleanor be safe. But let there be some foul play, too. Don't let her just be drunk."

When the telephone rang, Mother beat me to it. It was her Uncle Henry; he wanted to speak to Henry Carter directly. So Mother and I had to sit and wait beside that humming fan while Henry Carter leaned against the wall with the phone pressed to his ear.

Finally he heaved a sigh and said "Well, tell them I appreciate everything they've done. And ask them to get Eleanor to call me when she gets off at Atlanta. And, Uncle Henry, please make sure the porter actually puts her on a Northbound train this time."

Eleanor would not be getting into Richmond until tomorrow morning, Henry Carter told us. So Mother called *my* Uncle Henry, who was her older brother, and arranged for him to drive Henry Carter's mother, Aunt Min, and his sister Polly down from Charlottesville to see him.

They got to our house in time for a late dinner. And we had a good time eating fried chicken, corn pudding, black-eyed peas and stewed tomatoes — all the things that Mother could remember Henry Carter liked. Afterwards, the grownups reared back in their chairs and started swapping stories about Willoughby Spit where we used to spend the summers in cottages one lot apart.

Grandma had the cottage that we — Mother and my Uncle Henry as well as Mother's other brother and her sisters and the children — stayed in. And Grandma's brother Henry, who was Mother's Uncle Henry, had the cottage two lots up the beach where the others stayed.

When everybody got together, there were just too many Henrys. Especially since each one had a son who was called "Little Henry" with a tag to keep him straight, like "my Uncle Henry's Little Henry," or your brother Henry's Little Henry."

After World War II, those Little Henrys produced sons

who were called "Baby Henry," with even longer tags: "My Uncle Henry's Little Henry's Baby Henry." And those tags are used today although two of the Baby Henrys are over six feet tall and have sons of their own for whom the family has reverted to the simple name, "Henry." With a designating tag preceding it, of course: "My brother Henry's Little Henry's Baby Henry's Henry."

Even then, in 1943, it could get right complicated when Grandma's brother Henry had a crowd of other Henrys staying at his cottage. The same cottage, in fact where Eleanor had been spending the past week with Sarah Hartley — Mother's Uncle Henry's daughter. The one who had put Eleanor, or as my Uncle Henry said, more likely poured her on the Pocahontas that morning.

I had seen Sarah Hartley lace her breakfast grapefruit with a jigger full of bourbon so I could understand why her father might suspect that Eleanor, her guest, would be drunk at 10 a.m.

Well, I laughed until my ribs began to ache, as I listened to these stories at the dinner table there with Henry Carter. I'd heard most of them before, but then you never know when somebody is going to add some new detail that will turn the thing around completely.

Tonight they told about the hurricane of '33 and the time in Prohibition when my father brought some friends from Richmond down to Willoughby and they nearly died of boredom till they noticed that my grandfather kept a bottle labeled Gordon's Gin underneath the bow seat of his rowboat. So they asked him would he please take them fishing, though they hated to go fishing. And when he did, they had to spend two hours in the broiling sun on the Chesapeake Bay before he offered them a sip from his bottle. It turned out to be filled with drinking water. And they had at least another hour to go before he rowed them in.

After that, Henry Carter told about the time my mother went off to Virginia Beach "which Aunt Buff (that was his name for my grandmother) thought of as Sodom and Gomorrah. And she came back with a *big black eye...*"

Everybody started laughing then, because they knew the rest.

Still, my Uncle Henry added, "A black eye that she claimed she got riding the waves. Wasn't that the story, Bista?" This was his name for my mother. It means Big Sister? And then he imitated a shaky little voice, 'I was only floating in the ocean, Mother, when this big wave came along and turned my inner tube over. And the valve of it hit me in the eye.' "

"But Aunt Buff didn't ever *quite* believe her."

"Or let her go back to Virginia Beach till after she was married."

"Even then," my mother said, "it was safer not to let her know where I was going."

By the time the lemon pie came in, they had worked back to their school days in Norfolk where they had all grown up on the same block of Duke Street. And I began to notice there were certain Norfolk stories that they didn't tell this time.

The ones about poor Uncle Lawton who used to go on binges and kept losing his jobs, until, finally he lost the one that he was the best at — driving a streetcar on the Cottage Line from Willoughby to Norfolk. Of all the grownups in the family, he was the one the children loved the most, my mother said. And she never would forget that day she went to Sunday dinner at her grandfather's, the original Henry's house — where Aunt Min and Uncle Lawton came to live after he'd lost all his jobs in Fauquier County — and Mother asked, "Where's Uncle Lawton?" And nobody would answer.

Years later, she found out that Aunt Min had thrown him out.

The same shriveled Aunt Min who was sitting at the table, here in Richmond, with us now. So that meant Uncle Lawton would be Henry Carter's father. And Polly's father, too. Where is he now?" I wondered.

Likewise no one told about the time that Henry Carter brought that tacky first wife back to Norfolk — with a very nearly illegitimate son. And who nobody liked, and she took revenge by shouting like a fishwife to the baby in the backyard, "Henry Marshall! You come here this minute! Do you hear me, Henry Marshall? Or I'm gonna whip the living daylights out of you." In case the whole of Norfolk didn't know already just how far down the family had sunk.

That wife, thank the Lord, was now out of the picture. And Eleanor, though often drunk, was better born.

By the time they got their coffee, they had worked from high school up to V.M.I. and the time my mother's younger brother Sam coaxed a cow up two flights of stairs on the stoop there, and the superintendent had to hire a crane to get it down.

They were just about ready to go back to Fauquier County, and the even wilder stories about the days of Reconstruction and the summers they had spent in the musty clapboard houses that their parents — both sets of them, the women, too, named Marshall from their birth and married to their cousins — had grown up poor as church mice in.

But suddenly my mother interrupted.

"Now come on, Henry Carter. Can't you give us just a hint about your special Mission?"

I was shocked that she could be so unpatriotic. Hadn't she read the warnings posted all over the Post Office: "Don't ask your loved ones to reveal secret information." Didn't Mother understand that "The slip of a lip can sink a ship?"

But Henry Carter didn't seem to mind. He spread his fat, cigar-shaped fingers on the table, reared back in his creaky chair and said, "I'll tell you all about it if you'll promise me *two things*. First, you won't repeat it...

"No, we won't repeat a word."

"And second, you won't laugh."

"How can we promise that?"

"Is it enough if we promise that we'll try?"

That was enough, he said, and proceeded to tell how there was this brand of tobacco called Indian Chew made right here in Richmond by Commonwealth Tobacco. And the natives in New Guinea absolutely loved it. So the Army used it all the time to bribe them into telling where the Japanese were hiding.

Then, suddenly, last month, the company announced that it was going to stop production of Indian Chew, not knowing they would jeopardize the War in the Pacific. So Henry Carter did "what anybody else in this family would do. "I sent a cablegram to Uncle Henry. And sure enough, he came through with an airplane to fly me back here for a meeting with the officers of Commonwealth Tobacco. Tomorrow morning I'm to go there and apprise them of their patriotic duty to keep on making plugs of Indian Chew."

At that point Mother noticed me, "Good heavens. It's a school night! Why aren't you in bed?"

Half an hour later, I was in bed, listening to the radio I hid under the covers and doing long division by the light that was glowing from its tubes.

They were playing my favorite on the Hit Parade that week: "*You'll never knooow just how much I love you./ You'll never knooow just how much I care....*" when the telephone rang and I had to turn it off to hear my mother's voice downstairs:

"Henry Carter, it's Eleanor! Calling from Atlanta."

The next thing I heard was slow, heavy footsteps coming up the stairs. He was taking the call on the upstairs extension, in the bedroom next to mine.

In my life, I've never heard a man any madder at a woman than Henry Carter was at Eleanor that night. It made my stomach hurt to hear the way he bawled her out.

After he hung up the phone there was silence for a minute; and I started feeling sorry for him, sitting on the bed, feeling just as sad as I was that he'd gone and lost his temper at the wife he hadn't seen for two long years.

Then I heard somebody knocking on his door and a woman's voice so faint I had to get out of my bed and stretch out on the floor to hear it was his sister, Polly, asking, "Is Eleanor all right?"

"As right as she will ever be," said Henry Carter. "They've put her on a Pullman that gets into Richmond at eight twenty-five tomorrow morning."

"We've got to drive on back to Charlottesville tonight," Polly said. "But please give Eleanor my love. And one more thing, before we go downstairs. Have you heard any news about little Henry?"

Oh dear Lord. That meant *his* son Henry. By that first wife nobody liked. He was 19 years old and in the Navy now. And already he was Missing in Action.

"Yes, said Henry Carter. "They found his body with two others. Frozen in a life raft floating in the north Atlantic."

It was a long time before I got to sleep that night. Though I'd never seen this cousin, he was my blood kin. And only ten years older. And I could feel how it would be to be freezing in a life raft — first your fingers and your toes go numb, and then your arms and legs, and all the while the rubber raft is wet and the rough, dark waves of the North Atlantic are rising up on either side of you like snow-capped mountains.

The end of the line, I thought. There'll never be a Baby Henry Carter.

* * * *

As soon as I stepped onto the playground the next morning, my friends swung down from the jungle gym, and ran over to me shouting,

"Did he come?"

"Did the General with the Secret Mission come?"

"Yes," I said.

"Was he handsome?"

"Kind of, Also fat."

"And what about his wife?"

"Was she fat, too?"

"Or beautiful?"

"Did they kiss hard when they met?"

"Did they do it in the guest room?"

"She missed her train," I said. "I never got to see her."

They turned around and walked back to the jungle gym then. All except Weezie, who asked, "Did you hear what happened yesterday? On 'Mary Noble Backstage Wife'?"

"No," I said glumly.

"She finally saw him."

"Yeah?" I said. In spite of everything, I felt a weak stirring of interest. "And what'd she do?"

"Fainted," Weezie said. "But we expect she will come to this afternoon."

APPENDIX

ACKNOWLEDGMENTS

First and foremost I want to thank Beverly Nelson, my friend and fellow resident at Westminster Canterbury Richmond, for focusing her enormous talents as editor and designer on the publication of this book. It is her second "pandemic project" to raise money for the WCR Foundation. From the start, its main purpose has been to focus our thoughts and energy on something positive *beyond* the restrictions, threats and tragedies of COVID-19 that surrounded us in 2020-21.

I am also grateful to a gifted local artist, Louise Gilbert Freeman, who is also my daughter-in-law. On successive Sunday afternoons she has taken time off from her work in watercolor and oil painting to create superb minimalist line drawings that suggest but never intrude upon the stories that follow them.

In addition I need to express my gratitude to a stellar group of editors and writers: Kitty Williams, Marty Taylor, Elizabeth Morgan and Taylor Reveley III for their insightful comments on my work as well as editorial suggestions. Finally I would like to thank my friend and neighbor, Nancy Krider, for combing through the manuscript to correct mistakes we had missed before we sent it to the publisher, Dementi Milestone Publishing.

Wayne Dementi and his designer, Jayne Hushen, will now guide the electronic presentation of the text and illustrations through processes of printing, marketing and sales as yet unknown to us.

AUTHOR'S NOTE

When I was racking my brain to find a title for this collection of 10 stories, first published 30 to 60 years ago, "The Girl Who Was No Kin to the Marshalls" kept popping to the surface. I kept pushing it down. Did I really want to tie the whole collection to the limited perspective of a single story?

My graphic designer said the title was too long. Hard to work with on the jacket. Why not choose something more succinct? "The Gift and Other Stories?" Right away, I knew that wouldn't do. It didn't sound like me. Moreover, no one who has ever heard me try to tell a story would use the word "succinct" to describe the process.

But that other word, "kin," kept working like a fishhook in my mind, dragging that slightly snobbish, old-fashioned title to the surface so relentlessly that finally I gave up and decided to use it.

Now in the dusk of my own life, at age 87, I begin to see these stories in a new way: as bittersweet elegies to the story-telling habits of an enormous family in the mid-Twentieth-Century South. Through spontaneous narratives at family gatherings, in spite of the blind spots that concern us so today, the grownups managed to create a cocoon of love and laughter for their children — including my sister and myself and several hundred cousins in Virginia — to grow up in.

Though we did not know it at the time, we were being offered a priceless gift: a chance to observe and, with luck, develop in ourselves, a capacity to embrace and *enjoy* a wild variety of personalities and opinions before we broke away into the wider world.

The stories in this book, then, are the stories that a long-ago girl, the one who actually was kin to the Marshalls, would tell when she grew up to be a writer.

Style Weekly, June 24,1997
by ANNE HOBSON FREEMAN

WILLOUGHBY SPIT

When my great-grandfather died in 1914, he left each of his children several thousand dollars. Some say it was three thousand, others say five, but either sum would have been a windfall to my grandmother. She had five children then, ranging from age 3 to age 15, and a soft-hearted husband whose future at the Bank of Tidewater, in Portsmouth, was limited by the fact that he couldn't bear to foreclose mortgages. Instead, he'd try to find a friend, or even dig into his own almost empty pockets, to come up with the money to solve the mortgagee's immediate crisis.

So what did Grandma do with her inheritance? The only significant amount of cash that would ever come her way? She invested it, of course, immediately, in a summer cottage on Willoughby Spit at the mouth of the Chesapeake Bay.

Her father's dying words to her had been: "Try to keep the family together." By that he meant not only her children but also her older sister, and the four younger brothers she had helped him raise. And, of course, their children and their children's children.

Anne Hobson Freeman, 1940

One of her brothers bought the only other cottage on that block — if you can call two acres of sand and sea grass and splintered boardwalk stretching to the streetcar tracks a "block." And back and forth between those two cottages and around their two porches at least three generations of Marshall cousins ran.

By the time I got there, the cottages had just barely survived the Hurricane of '33 — which I experienced in *utero* and re-experienced each summer as my uncles and aunts sat rocking on one porch or

Strib Marshall, Anne Freeman's grandfather,
relaxing on the porch at Willoughby

the other, nursing their highballs and adding new details to the story of that night. How the wild waters from the Chesapeake rose up to the streetcar tracks, while my grandfather insisted it was just a bad Northeaster and how the family finally had to be evacuated, in three row boats and a Black Maria.

Most summers we would drive down from Richmond in mid-June and stay through Labor Day, since my mother was her mother's chief assistant. And each year I'd be surprised, all over again, by the sudden salty taste in the air when my father rolled his window down at the Old Point Comfort ferry.

The first night, lying in my cot, I would listen intently to the waves flapping on the sand, just beyond the open windows, and stay awake to watch the long finger of light from the Thimble Shoal lighthouse slide around the bare walls of the girls' bedroom.

My biggest worry always was: What kind of sheet have I been given? An old one and a thin one, that's for certain. But is it one of those that has a tiny hole which your toe will catch in the middle of the night and wake you to the dreadful sound of ripping cloth? You draw your legs up tight to avoid further damage, but your body soon forgets and straightens out. And then the awful ripping sound wakes you again.

By the time the sky beyond the screen turns rosy-pink and a flat red sun pops out of the water, you find that one whole leg is exposed, while long pieces of the sheet are lying on either side of it.

Grandma tries to be a good sport when you hand the strips of sheet to her. "We'll get some good dust rags out of this," she says. But you've seen the calendar in the kitchen with the Chessie cat sleeping on a soft white pillow and the names of all the aunts, uncles and cousins scrawled across the dates on which they'll be arriving. And you know she must be thinking, "Will the supply of sheets make it through the summer?"

Towels were a problem, too. And screen doors which we younger ones kept busting through in our eagerness to catch up with the older cousins who were always running off to do something so extremely adult and exotic that they didn't want the younger cousins horning in on it. If a screen could not be patched, we were allowed to tear it apart, strand by strand, then twist the strands into a single wire, which — when a Dixie cup was attached at either end — became a private telephone from the girls' room to the boys'.

At that stage of my life, I didn't know much about boys. The first one I had ever seen in his naked entirety was a four-year-old cousin, screaming bloody murder at the top of the steps, while Grandma and my mother stripped his sandy bathing suit off and slapped handfuls of baking soda on the bright red blotches where a stinging nettle got him.

Grandma's porch had a swing with dark green slats. Three or four cousins could sit there and sing all of the songs they'd ever learned. But when the whole crowd got together, we used Uncle Richard's porch next door, with its huge metal glider and wicker chairs.

Best of all was the beach. Sometimes the grownups would scoop out a pit there and build a fire for a marshmallow roast. The trick was to pierce the white blob firmly in the center with the tip of your untwisted coat hanger, then hold it at exactly the right distance from the flame, so that it would turn gently brown, not black, on the outside and still run soft and gooey at the center.

We roasted hot dogs, too, or "wienies" as we called them, and ears of corn, still in their husks, and the fresh fish — spot or croaker — that our uncles had caught from the wooden row boat we helped them drag down to the water early in the morning and summoned back for lunch by ringing a brass bell and waving dish towels on the porch.

As the summer progressed, the bottoms of our feet grew tough enough to take us a full mile down the road to a store that sold jawbreakers and licorice sticks and orange popsicles which we would break in half and race to finish eating before they melted down our arms.

Once a summer we'd be taken all the way to Ocean View to buy pink clouds of cotton candy and watch the older cousins ride the rickety white latticed roller coaster, which everybody I knew called the "leap de dips."

The saddest end of summer I remember was 1939, when at the breakfast table, one mild September morning, my almost always jolly grandfather turned suddenly terrifyingly solemn as the radio began to tell about some German soldiers marching into some fairy-tale sounding country I'd never heard about before.

Through most of World War II, our summers at Willoughby continued almost as they had before, though I think even the youngest children sensed that we were playing at the edge of some disaster. Ugly submarine nets had been strung out into the bay only five or six jetties up the beach from us. Mother's favorite first cousin's husband spent most of his vacation on the porch, with binoculars focused on the water for the tell-tale periscope that would indicate a U-Boat. One afternoon he actually saw one and leapt up from his rocking chair and ran into the house to telephone the Navy. And everybody, on both porches, saw the British destroyer gliding into Hampton Roads with thick black smoke pouring from its turrets.

One day we even caught a glimpse of FDR himself, in the back seat of an open car, riding in a motorcade from the ferry to the naval base. And he waved at me — I still maintain it was at *me* — as I sat watching from the back steps of our cottage with my older sister and seven of my cousins.

A week before VE Day, Grandma Marshall died. And nobody in the family had the heart, or maybe it was energy, or simply inclination to open up the cottage at Willoughby without her. And so, eventually, my grandfather sold it. And I went off to summer camp in the Allegheny Mountains.

Now and then I think about my grandmother's inheritance. Suppose she had invested those 1914 dollars differently? In U.S. Steel, perhaps or Coca-Cola stock. If so, this much I know: we, her descendants, would not be where we find ourselves today, among the very rich in kissing kin and summer memories. □